LONDON

AFTER A FASHION

LONDON
AFTER A FASHION

ALISTAIR O'NEILL

REAKTION BOOKS

Published by Reaktion Books Ltd
33 Great Sutton Street
London ec1v 0dx, uk

www.reaktionbooks.co.uk

First published 2007
Copyright © Alistair O'Neill, 2007

Supported by

 Arts & Humanities
Research Council

Printed and bound in Great Britain by Cromwell Press, Trowbridge, Wiltshire

British Library Cataloguing in Publication Data
O'Neill, Alistair
    London: after a fashion
    1. Fashion – England – London – History – 19th century
    2. Fashion – England – London – History – 20th century
    3. London (England) – Social life and customs - 19th century
    4. London (England) – Social life and customs – 20th century
    I. Title
    391.009421'09034

    ISBN–13: 978 1 86189 315 4
    ISBN–10: 1 86189 315 9

CONTENTS

From Paul Kelly and Kieran Evans's film *Finisterre*, 2003.

In November 2003 the British pop band Saint Etienne hosted a double-bill screening at the Barbican Cinema in London of their short film Finisterre (also the name of their recently released album), and its point of inspiration, the rarely seen documentary of 1967, The London Nobody Knows, directed by Norman Cohen. The documentary had a precedent in Geoffrey Fletcher's travel guide The London Nobody Knows (1962), a collection of calligraphic illustrations and written anecdotes about the capital formed from his earlier regular column in the Daily Telegraph. Seen from a historical distance, as is the case for many of Saint Etienne's inspirations, the film adaptation suggested to the pop band not only a bygone vision of the capital, but one that challenged many common-held assumptions about the representation of the city at certain points of transition. As a band member, Bob Stanley, noted:

> Carnaby chicks and chaps, the 1967 we have been led to remember, are shockingly juxtaposed with feral meths drinkers, filthy shoeless kids, squalid Victoriana. Camden Town still resembles the world of Walter Sickert. There is romance and adventure, but mostly there is malnourishment. London looks like a shithole.[1]

This is a vision of London rendered incoherent by virtue of its extreme juxtapositions. It challenges our view of a late 1960s London vibrant with youth and colour in the shopping district of Carnaby Street. Instead, we are given a handful of worn and austere fragments shot under a grey skyline for us to cast our eyes over. Camden Town is yet to become a shopping area for the second-hand and sub-cultural. Instead, it shows the scars of its music-hall days and, indeed, its murders from the turn of the twentieth century; and these historical references collide with the modern-day grime of the area.

This historical medley echoes both the cinematic metaphor of montage and Walter Benjamin's idea of understanding the city through montage. More than any other writer, Benjamin remains central to a contemporary understanding of the modern city in cultural and historical terms, and his rendering of the city suggests that the arrangement of these historical picture-scenes in the topography of the metropolis inevitably relay something of the present.

This is something that M. Christine Boyer crystallized in her book *The City of Collective Memory*, where 'each fragment becomes a static tableau of the city, representing contrasting views made more explicit by their proximity to each other . . . yet each conveys some nuance of contemporary times'.[2] This conveying of the contemporary is also illustrated by the film *Finisterre*, which transposed the earlier documentary's visual sense of historical discontinuity across the fabric of contemporary London. So, instead of mourning the loss of Victorian oyster rooms and Edwardian public conveniences, it wanted to raise awareness about the plight of the post-war Italian cafés, such as The New Piccadilly on Denman Street, near Piccadilly Circus, that were the setting for the beginnings of British pop culture in the 1950s.

These films are tinged with the attitudes towards the past of their day. Both focus on what has been lost and what has survived. But whereas Fletcher and Cohen bemoaned the onslaught of office-block modernism and glass curtain walls, Saint Etienne film the post-war housing blocks of Farringdon with the loving attention of those interested in the reawakened potential of modernism as a choice for inner-city living at the beginning of the twenty-first century. What these very different

From Norman Cohen's film *The London Nobody Knows*, 1967.

accounts have in common is the way in which fashion – as a vehicle of change – propels the multifarious attitudes and beliefs that shape the evolving fabric of London.

Both films share a position that is populist in spirit but resistant to consensual opinion, particularly in their disregard for official accounts of London's history. Walter Benjamin also believed that these official kinds of history writing were bogus, seeing them as reconstructing fragmented events in a fabricated architecture. He believed that random objects from the historical past should collide with others found in the contemporary in order to give insight to the present and offer a critical understanding of what had gone before, offering an alternative form of history. So his study of the shopping arcades of nineteenth-century Paris was a means by which to understand the consumer dream worlds of the twentieth; the debris of the Victorian flea markets and the role of the rag-picker were the material through which to grasp

From Cohen's *The London Nobody Knows.*

Mark and Syrie, July 1985, London.

the economic transformation of modern commodities – how they are bought and sold, and how their symbolic value changes in this exchange.

In a similar vein, both films about London show visually rich collisions that salvage the history of the city in the present, thereby agitating our understanding of the history of the city as a chronology. This book locates the practices and expressions of fashion across the span of twentieth-century London through a similar methodology. Like Benjamin's remnant objects of study from nineteenth-century Paris, the vestiges of fashionable London in the twentieth century are drawn from the study of fashionable districts and shopping areas, the circulation of goods across the markets of the capital, the recycling of ideas from past ages, and the role of the stylist – the modern-day rag-picker, who possesses the ability to transform goods and ideas through the projection of fashion.

This connection between the nineteenth-century rag-picker and the creative practitioner in the field of fashion was first made by Caroline Evans in her discussion of the Belgian designer Martin Margiela, and consequently in the scavenging aesthetic of styling found in i-D *Magazine* in the 1980s and British catwalk fashion in the 1990s.[3] My identification of the stylist is drawn from an earlier definition by Jonathan Raban in his book *Soft City* (1974), where he claimed that metropolitan arbiters of style (the kind of individuals that we might not identify today as stylists) are entrepreneurs whose activities are defined by what he termed the 'Moroccan birdcage syndrome'. By this he meant a tendency for individuals to transform the economic and symbolic potential of commodities from worthless things into objects of desire, thought of as fashionable. The example he used was a shop around the corner from where he lived in London that sold Moroccan birdcages painted white, not to contain birds but as tasteful decorative objects for fashionable interiors of the early 1970s. Raban claimed it as:

A useful model for a certain kind of industrial process – a process which both supplies a demand for commodities whose sole feature is their expressiveness of taste, and becomes, by virtue of its laws of economic transformation, the ultimate arbiter of that taste. The stylistic entrepreneurs who make their living out of this curious trade go, along with gangsters and dandies, into the bracket of people possessed of a special kind of city knowledge.[4]

All the practitioners considered in this book are similarly defined by how they project their own vision of fashionability through their individual sense of city knowledge. Their production and projection of fashion, style and taste expresses their cultural capital (as in Pierre Bordieu's definition). But, more importantly, it also expresses their 'cultural capital of capital culture'. By this I mean that their social demonstration of taste is not only performed in the metropolis, but it is also informed by it. As Raban suggests, by the categorizing of the stylist with the gangster and the dandy, these are people who navigate the city in ways that resist or deviate from prescribed routes and accepted practices (such as the Francis Bacon's night walks through London in the guise of a gangster in leather), and it is this understanding of the city that forces ingenuity and invention. Raban was adept at realizing that these individuals are not only possessed of this special kind of city knowledge but also become landmarks in the city themselves, signs by which we recognize and navigate our own routes:

> This is one of the most important ways in which the city becomes legible. To the newcomer who has not learned its language, a large city is a chaos of details, a vast Woolworth's store of differently coloured, similarly priced objects. Yet, just as there are consecrated routes through its labyrinth of streets, so the welter of commodities is ordered by patterns of human usage. They are arranged in clusters around particular personalities; a velvet suit, a string of pearls, a furled umbrella, a watch-chain, a caftan, an ivory cigarette-holder, each belongs to a conventionally established 'character', and the adept city-dweller is engaged in the constant manipulation of these stylistic qualities, continuously relating his self-presentation to his audience through the medium of such expressive objects.[5]

The chaos of details in London, then, is not merely the maze of its topo-logical arrangement and the cornucopia of commodities drawn from the present and the past, but how these are networked by the human interaction of movement and consumption. It is the dextrous use of these inter-relations that is crucial to the creativity of London life, for those with the gift are central figures in shaping fashionable attitudes that impact and reverberate upon the evolution of the capital.

If there is a figure, albeit an extreme one, that galvanizes this con-cept, it is the beguiling vision of the Surrealist artist Sheila Legge dressed as the Surrealist Phantom, her head covered in rose blooms standing in the middle of Trafalgar Square in 1936. Her incongruous juxtaposition amongst the familiar landscape of lion heads, pigeons and the façade of the National Gallery claims her as a surreal landmark of London: a stand-in for the figure of Nelson on his column, as if it were implicitly understood by the birds that rest on her arms. The power of this image, primarily intended to promote the cause of Surrealism but also, in its own right, an extreme statement of fashion-able identity, was later reworked by Leigh Bowery in the 1990s as one of his elaborate costumes of the night worn at Kinky Gerlinky, a club night at Maximus Discotheque, further up the Charing Cross Road in Leicester Square. The motif of the material-covered head subsequently reappeared in a collection by Alexander McQueen from A/W 1998/9 in scarlet red floral lace. Thus the floriated figure inhabits different bodies at differ-ent historical moments in fashionable London. And its reappearance is bound by its disappearances.

For all of these individuals, who can all be identified as stylists in their own ways, the use of the motif is largely unconcerned with origin-ality (as we shall later find out, it is lifted from a fantastical figure in a painting by Salvador Dalí). Rather, its deployment contradicts the logic of what underpins a fashionable metropolitan identity. By this I mean that the practice of fashionable metropolitan activity should be about the attuning of all senses to the tempo of city life. In the complete cov-ering of the head, the vision suggests that the individual is unable to navigate the city – by being deaf, dumb and blind to its maelstrom. And yet the metaphorical suggestion is that the figure does move through

Sheila Legge as 'phantom mannequin' in Trafalgar Square, 1936 (possibly by Claude Cahun).

Fergus Greer, Leigh Bowery, 'Session 11 / Look 10 / July 1989'.

Alexander McQueen, A/W 1998/99.

the city: guided by its intuition it wanders, phantom-like, through both the actual city and the history of the city, excavating disorienting visions to disturb the idea of London fashion through the very processes of trawling the capital's history of fashionable identities. The figure operates as a key from the past to unlock the present.

Even though this interpretation of a fashionable identity in London may seem fanciful, the principle of a visual quotation of fashion reverberating through the time and space of the city is not that unusual. Iain Chambers identified it in the disjuncture of street life, 'a world at once removed from daily routines, where our clothes, our bodies, our faces become quotations, drawn from the other, imaginary side of life: from fashion, the cinema, advertising and the infinite suggestions of metropolitan iconography'.[6] Chambers stresses that it is not necessarily what we project that is important, but how this relates to the spaces between the projections, how metropolitan fashionability as a random mix of fragmented, free-floating quotations is equally informed by the fragmented spaces of the city.

Indeed, it is these spaces that have fostered fashion's own capacity for collage. Collage is a modernist art stratagem that dislocates reality by reducing it to a series of surfaces that are then arranged in an illogical manner; overlay it with Benjamin's notion of the fragment found in the context of the city and you have an understanding of the topography of the city as being in a continual and complex state of dissonance and flux. It emphasizes the transitory qualities of things designed, produced and sold as ephemera, but which stubbornly persist in the fabric of the city as visual traces of earlier times. Most potently, it evokes the state of fragmentation as an indicator of the experience of modernity in the city.

This was identified as early as 1903 by Georg Simmel, who claimed that metropolitan life intensified the sense of individuality through exposure to its fast-paced and rhythmical stimuli. Simmel believed that fashion not only matched this pace, but was also an indicator of individual perception, since 'few phenomena of social life possess such a pointed curve of consciousness as does fashion'.[7] In claiming fashion as central to, and expressive of, metropolitan life, Simmel, as well as others since, have continued to stress the importance of fashion for identification and navigation within the city.

Raban regarded his stylists and their things as the soft attributes of the city that we navigate through from eye level. His 'Soft City' was in opposition to the hard attributes of structures and maps such as the bird's eye view of the city. The sociologist Michel de Certeau also recognized that these different ways of understanding the city, one visceral, one semi-abstracted, were wholly different. He claimed the everyday experience of the street as being more unusual than the totalizing vision of 'seeing the whole' of the city from above, and that in their criss-crossing of the city, its inhabitants produce 'an urban "text" they write without being able to read':

> The networks of these moving, intersecting writings compose a manifold story that had neither author nor spectator, shaped out of fragments of trajectories and alterations of spaces: in relation to representations, it remains daily and indefinitely other.[8]

Much of what we might identify as London fashion is formed from this kind of manifold story; as a text it is informed by similar intersections that conjure representations wholly removed from the realm of the everyday. The problem remains in the area of 'reading' this text. Much of what has been written about the relation between London and fashion is interested only in presenting the totalizing vision of a bird's eye view, with little regard for understanding it as a situated practice at eye level. Representations that are more often than not visual examples of this relation often become cast as mythical substitutes that 'explain' the relation by their survival alone. Little examination is ever given over to reconfiguring the networks of connections that once plotted the coordinates and then produced such representations.

But how do we chart these fashions, these pathways and these identities? What mapping devices can we use to define historically the 'soft city' of fashion in London? And is a cultural topography of fashion in London in any way possible? Yes it is, and one could chart a relationship between fashionable identities and the historical era of twentieth-century

A 19th-century fan printed with a plan of the capital.

London if one posits an alternative concept of cultural mapping that is able to embrace, plot and identify eye-level activity.

First and foremost, the use of a map to understand the fashionable districts of London is nothing new, from the 'Swinging Guide to London' printed in *Time* magazine in July 1966 to the map in Andrew Tucker's *The London Fashion Book* (1998). These visual pictorializations of time and space often appear when London is credited with experiencing a creative high point in global terms. Yet they also succeed in overlaying a tourist sensibility upon the features of the map, so that the fashionable experiences represented are pre-digested and prescribed with little in the way of the deviation or exploration that I have already identified as crucial to the production of fashionability. Although they function as useful historical snapshots of the geographical spread of the London fashion scene in the age of Swinging London or Cool Britannia, the historical factors that account for the sedimentation or shift in the location of fashionable identities in London remain beyond the scope of pictorial definition.

To make sense of the idea of cultural mapping I am interested in, I want to consider a much earlier map of fashionable London from the early part of the nineteenth century, printed on the side of a ladies' fan that as an object transforms factual mapping into fashionable decoration. As with the two previous examples, all celebrate a simplified vision of the city with an emphasis on fashionable sights and structures that might not otherwise appear in official maps of the city (this fan includes a list of the best places from which to hail a carriage). This is often achieved by compressing the space between monuments, reconfiguring the topology into an idealized vision or prospect, a practice that strongly relates to the time of the Grand Tour in the eighteenth century, when these kinds of maps were known as *capriccio*.

What I especially like about the fan is its ability to problematize the notion of the map as a rigidly defined structure. First, its dual purpose as map and fan means that the look of the thing when seen is unlikely to be fixed; instead, it will oscillate wildly, visually challenging the permanence of its printed coordinates. Secondly, when the fan is closed, the map is pleated and the distances between the referents are further compressed, offering a different logic to their arrangement, destabilizing the actual experience of the geography. Therefore the fan is a useful metaphor to explain how historical accounts of fashion in London as an expressive aspect of modernity can benefit from an analysis that pleats time and space into a multiplicity of historical eras defined through geographical referents. In evoking the actual experience of geography at eye level it is also able to contain something of the strange deviations from accepted practices and routes that characterize the individuals who wander the city possessed of a special kind of knowledge.

This methodology is also quite similar to something that the cultural geographers Steve Pile and Nigel Thrift have identified in their attempt to map the modern subject in the city as *wayfinding*: a procedure of 'visiting in turn all, or most, of the positions one takes to constitute the field . . . [covering] descriptively as much of the terrain as possible, exploring it on foot rather than looking down at it from an airplane'.[9] This strategy for cultural mapping is perhaps more widely understood in relation to London through the writings of Iain Sinclair that document his arterial and atypical journeys across the man-made fabric of London, or in Patrick Keiller's fictional character Robinson, meandering through similar terrain in the films *London* (1994) and *Robinson in Space* (1997).

Like Sinclair's books and all the films about London I have mentioned, this book charts a twentieth-century story of the city that takes an unusual route as its starting point, challenging histories of fashionable London by presenting them from a perspective that makes them appear strange and unfamiliar. It is a journey of instances that have caught my attention, made me wonder why such a manifestation occurred, why it remains overlooked, or why attention has been carelessly lavished on it. I want to show rare finds hidden in the history of fashionable London – finds that if not already extinct are on the cusp of being so. Other finds are differently disguised as official versions of this history. These I wish to re-examine to show how they are necessarily more complex than how we might currently understand them. I want to question why so many gaps and lacunae in the history remain and ask why it is important to attend to these omissions.

We begin in London, but in a West End tattoo parlour and Turkish bath house that are gateways to elsewhere. They mark the late nineteenth-century interest in exotic otherness and in the display of the tattooed body as an indicator of worldliness. The body as the site of fashionable display continued at the turn of the century in the variety theatre and fashion houses of the West End, where the presentation of flesh-coloured fabric as an effect of bare skin was a means of projecting the erotic potential of women as bearers of commodities. We then turn to women Surrealists who in the 1930s challenged this fusing of femininity and commodity culture through their adoption of the fashionably surreal hat as a strategy of their own artistic identity. The self-constructed artistic identity then carries into post-war Soho, with Francis Bacon and his acquaintances, who promoted a purposefully sordid and stained form of attire in contempt of fashion. This is then balanced by the entrepreneur John Stephen, who awoke men to the possibilities of a self-conscious and smart fashionability on Carnaby Street. It is followed by the very different retailing exploits in the King's Road of the 1970s, which were to prove to be central to Carnaby Street's downfall. We then walk again down the King's Road, seemingly taking a step backwards in our pursuit of flower power, but actually concerned with the fashionable marketing of chintz in the 1980s and the blossoming gentrification of Chelsea and Covent Garden. The final chapter, dealing with the re-articulation of the East End as a setting for fashionable identities in the 1990s, shifts us across the East–West axis of the capital to consider a conception of London as a wasteland where ingenuity is formed from a poverty of materials.

The examples I have chosen are all defined by a journey that a narrator takes across the capital. Although it resembles an actual physical journey, the pathways taken are unorthodox and the narrative deviates many times from a direct route – breaking, doubling-back on itself, moving into different epochs, loitering for no known reason. As a strategy it well suits the examination of fashion, in that fashion too moves in equally unpredictable directions, dictated by the vagaries of whim and fancy. With its compulsion for historical recycling, fashion moves in similar pathways.

A small relic of this kind of history, found in one of my trawls of the city, reads: 'London's First Second Hand Boutique: Kinky, Period & Military Gear; Open Monday to Saturday'. Turning the card over reveals a delightful sketch of a slightly doubtful soldier bearing the name 'I was Lord Kitchener's Valet'. Contained here is all that we should savour about London and fashion: the irreverent take on history; the absurdity of claiming to be the first at second hand; the perversion in mixing different kinds of clothing up with their purpose; the salacious skewing of point of view, even the whiff of a Sunday tabloid story that will sell, sell, sell. This is commerce, but it is also creativity. This is London: After a Fashion.

In a similar vein, this attempt to map fashion in a history of twentieth-century London is not purely defined by the actual practice of way-finding

293 PORTOBELLO ROAD, W.10

LADBROKE 3826

Promotional card for the shop 'I Was Lord Kitchener's Valet', Portobello Road, 1960s.

across the capital; rather, it is also a form of way-finding across a terrain of surviving material culture, trawling and tracing the multiple inter-faces that once linked the people, practices and commodities together. It is a form of investigation that travels between the visible and above-ground world of fashion and the often hidden and below-ground world of the archive. Much of the research for the book has been concerned with calling up and inspecting what lies in London's many archives; reconsidering London's history as it unfurls from the roll of microfiche film, as it is pulled with white gloves out of acid-free tissue paper, as it slips from the file of correspondences or as it is found pasted into scrap-books as fragments of a once fashionable life. Sifting through the sediment of material recalls a world that seems distant and strange, an exoticism we find hard to relate to. Much of it reveals a London long-gone, a hidden London that nobody seemingly knows, but one that offers us material with which we can further embroider our own understanding of the city, as we map it in the geography of our minds.

In titling their film *Finisterre*, Saint Etienne wanted it to evoke the solitary pleasure of listening to the shipping forecast at night. For those at sea, the shipping forecast serves as an informative announcement of rational data, but for inner-city London listeners such as Bob Stanley it suggests a poetical recital imaginatively constructing an audible world of exotic names and indecipherable coordinates. This is underlined by the fact that the name Finisterre, a feature of the shipping forecast since 1949, was abandoned and renamed FitzRoy in 2002 in accordance with the United Nations World Meteorological Organization (WMO). In this book I hope to offer similar pleasures of the lost and found, reconfiguring the fabric of fashionable twentieth-century London as a compilation of coordinates and features that, in being scrutinized through a different lens, conjure a landscape that can illuminate and enrich our 'soft' sense of the capital we carry around with us:

> The city as we imagine it, the soft city of illusion, myth, aspiration, nightmare, is as real, maybe more real, that the hard city one can locate on maps in statistics, in monographs on urban sociology and demography and architecture.[10]

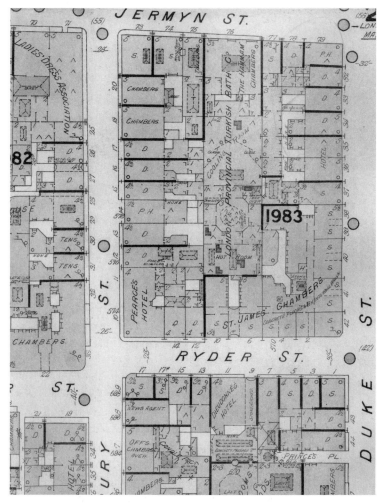

Fire Regulation Map showing part of Jermyn Street (London IX), March 1889.

CHAPTER ONE

To sit in Quaglino's restaurant in Mayfair today is to be happily immersed in the trappings of a pleasure palace. At the height of its revamp by Sir Terence Conran in the 1990s, an ashtray stolen from the restaurant was the ultimate, covert badge of belief in fashionable dining as a measure of success and excess in the capital. The practice was so widespread that an ashtray amnesty was organized as part of the restaurant's tenth anniversary celebrations in 2003, where they received more than 1,500 back (it is thought that they have actually lost in the region of 25,000). Quaglino's restaurant is actually much older, first opened by Giovanni Quaglino in 1929. When Conran found himself on a ladder gazing into a large cavernous hole behind a shop front on Bury Street in the early 1990s, he realized in the midst of the stench of the drains and the scattering of rats that he had stumbled on the former site of the original Quaglino's.

Little did he know that the space he resurrected was also part of the former site of a nineteenth-century Turkish bath house at 76 Jermyn Street, considered in its time to be the most famous in Europe. The Hammam, as it was known, was a wholly different kind of pleasure palace. Even more unusual is the fact that this Jermyn Street attraction included a tattoo parlour that was located in the same building. To have a tattoo from this parlour was not unlike the peculiar delight of smoking using a stolen ashtray: both were passing vogues that could be enjoyed only in private rather than through any form of public display; but more than this, it was because they celebrated an immoral, almost criminal sense of style at odds with the prevailing moral climate and its view of what constituted fashionable consumption.

An engraving of 'The Turkish Bath, Jermyn Street', from Walter Thornbury and Edward Walford, *Old and New London* (1897).

At the end of the nineteenth century in late Victorian London, a curious vogue for tattooing prevailed for a short time among the upper classes. Little evidence of this fashionable craze survives beyond the odd article extolling the peculiarities of London life that were regularly printed in the newly developing illustrated newspapers and magazines, many of which were just beginning to incorporate half-tone photographic illustrations. Although offering rare commentaries on this temporary trend for permanent designs on human skin, none of the articles readily explains why tattooing suddenly became a mark of fashion for the elite rather than just a mark of rank, class or profession

An engraving of the 'Turkish Bath (Jermyn Street): Cooling Room', from George R. Sims, *Living London* (1908).

An engraving of the 'Turkish Bath (Jermyn Street): Shampooing Room', from Sims's *Living London*.

for lesser souls. What the few surviving articles do illustrate is that the best way to promote the fashion for tattooing at the time was not to mention too much of its origins as a craft. As *The Strand* magazine noted:

> Turning over the leaves, we notice, amongst other quaint designs at this moment adorning the bodies of some of our best-known society men, three five-pound notes, full size, on which, perhaps, the owner can 'raise the wind', if at any time short of a cab-fare, by placing himself in temporary pawn; a fox hunt in full cry, horses and their scarlet-coated riders, with a very level pack of hounds careering down the owner's back in wild pursuit of a 'little red rascal', racing for his life; whilst one more than lucky individual who rumour says has an extremely tender epidermis, not content with a handsome pair of dark blue socks with scarlet 'clocks' on his feet, has lately been adorned with all manner of strange designs, from his neck down to the top of his socks, and this at quite a fabulous price, when we bear in mind the length of time it must have taken to carry out such a large order.[1]

This article recounts a visit a journalist made to the tattoo parlour of Sutherland Macdonald, situated within the same building as the Hammam Turkish baths in 1897. Even today, Jermyn Street remains the place where a man can buy the finest accessories to furnish his bespoke suit (hopefully for the one he has had made on Savile Row). The range of shirt makers, shoemakers, scent shops and snuff shops (many with a royal warrant) that have sold their wares since the mid-nineteenth century defines a gentlemanly code of sartorial respectability through the many trappings on offer. So the idea of a tattoo parlour offering a service that could bear a similar mark of distinction seems rather odd. The custom-designed cornucopia of motifs mentioned in the article is far removed from the conventional tattoo designs we recognize today, but then neither would they have been found in the anthropological accounts of tattooing amassed in pockets of Europe and America across the second half of the nineteenth century. In order to make sense of the

"'A Battle Royal in Mid-Air" – Macdonald's Masterpiece', from Gambier Bolton, 'Pictures on the Human Skin', in the *Strand Magazine*, 1897.

momentary appearance of these exotic and esoteric designs, it is worth applying the findings of these early anthropological studies to question how supposedly civilized men and women were driven to mark their bodies permanently with ornamental designs.

Cesar Lombroso's paper *The Criminal Man in Relation to Anthropology, Jurisprudence and Prison Discipline* (1878) was the first to study self-inflicted markings on criminals held in captivity. The study grafted a causal link between the tattoos of criminals and men of war with those of the primitive. Four years later Donald Fletcher from the Anthropological

Society of Washington published his paper 'Tattooing among Civilized People', where he expanded upon Lombroso's model by establishing a further three motives:

1. Vanity. A childish delight in the display of an ornament; the pleasure of being thought singular and original.
2. Imitation. This is, perhaps, the most prolific cause. A soldier who was rallied for his tattooed designs, replied, 'We are like sheep; we can't see anything done by a comrade without imitating it, even though it hurts us.'
3. Idleness; and to it must be attributed the prevalence of the custom among soldiers, sailors, criminals and prostitutes.[2]

The common findings of many of these studies were the unequivocal links made between cause and effect, motive and motif. Somewhat later, these findings were seized upon by the Viennese architect Adolf Loos as the evidence to support his moral belief in the removal of orna-mentation from architecture and utilitarian objects at the beginning of the twentieth century. His manifesto *Ornament and Crime* (1908) became central to the acceptance of modernism as an expression of modernity, refined taste and judgement by claiming that the need to ornament, be it a building or a body, was driven from a desire no different for that of a criminal or a degenerate: 'The modern man who tattoos himself is either a criminal or a degenerate . . . The tattooed who are not in prison are latent criminals or degenerate aristocrats.'[3]

Here we find rare mention of those upper-class English men writ-ten about in *The Strand*, and yet the reason for these men to partake in the 'art' of tattooing is not so clear. In the first instance, the designs offered by the tattooist Sutherland Macdonald do not readily fit into those categories identified by Lombroso; they are symbolic not so much of love, religion, war or profession, but a rather exclusive, even esoteric sense of leisure and pleasure. Secondly, the 'custom' of idleness is one that Fletcher was keen to stress as belonging only to those from the low-est social orders. To categorize 'some of our best-known society men' as practising exactly the same custom as that demonstrated by 'soldiers,

'Falcon, on the Author's Back, by Mr Sutherland Macdonald', from Bolton's 'Pictures on the Human Skin'.

'Snake, Tattooed in Green and Black, round the Author's Neck, by Mr Sutherland Macdonald', from Bolton's 'Pictures on the Human Skin'.

sailors, criminals and prostitutes' would seem perverse unless, of course, it was the fashionable intention. Given that the men received their tattoos in the same building that held a Turkish bath house, it is not unlikely that they may well have frequented the baths to bare the designs that sat proudly on their skins.

The daring tattoos that these men bore are best understood through their location in the space and time of the city, enriching how they were rendered and how they appeared on the body. So the £5 notes only make sense in the spare money one would raise to hail a cab; the hunting scene claims a love of the chase for the man about town who would really rather be in the country; and the elaborate designs on the man with the sensitive epidermis are measured by the cost of their time. The tattooed socks the man wears adorned with scarlet clocks are not necessarily an emblem of idleness, but are the literal and physical embodiment of 'filling time'. By this I mean that the London gent 'fills time' by wearing the bespoke socks that mark his movements in the city, indeed the movement of his feet, as ever aware of the passage of time. They also indicate how arduous an amount of time it must have taken to have these accoutrements made, while his sensitive skin would have ensured that the experience would have been far from idle: it was a way of 'filling-time' for aesthetic ends, literally to be branded by it. The gentleman evidently had to pay in more ways than one to take pleasure in bearing designs that were considered to be so very timely in their fashion.

This idea of having a tattoo to express the idea of 'filling-time' is also symptomatic of a wider condition of cultivated languor and self-conscious reflection, often termed decadence, that came to characterize the culture of *fin-de-siècle* London. Decadence as a literary and artistic movement in London most readily conjures the *Japonisme*-inspired, inked line drawings of Aubrey Beardsley, particularly in the provocative images he produced to advertise Oscar Wilde's theatrical productions. In his poster design for *Salome* (first reproduced as the cover to the inaugural issue of *The Studio* in 1893) we have the encapsulation of many themes relating to Decadence: the superiority of artifice or a staged effect over the 'natural'; a fascination with depravity; and a visual interest in extremity – all manifest in a corrupt capital. Beardsley's heightened stylizations of form may appear stark, but they never fail to delineate the excessive attributes of filigree and fine decoration (in a manner not unlike certain styles of tattooing). Just as Adolf Loos found tattooing a sign of moral degeneracy, his progressive followers would have held Beardsley's drawings in equal contempt.

This view of the time was informed by ideas about degeneration drawn from the fields of criminology and anthropology. They contributed to the argument that decadence as a cultural form of permissiveness fed the onslaught of moral degeneracy that threatened European civilization. A central figure in the advancing of these arguments from the field of psychiatry was Professor Cesar Lombroso. He would have been appalled at the idea that his work on tattooing amongst criminals was the inspiration for the fashionable elite to parade as depraved subjects of artifice, but it certainly demonstrates a link between the onslaught of decadence and the popularity of tattooing.

In many Decadent texts one finds early evidence of the modernist mode of mixing popular forms of expression with high cultural terms, and this is crucial to the notion of decadence as a mode of behaviour. In its outright rejection of bourgeois values, decadence embraced otherness in a number of ways. It could mean exoticism by country or even by class. For those less inclined to travel, the corrupt capital offered all manner of popular and lowly attractions that offered the cultivation of exotic experiences. In a sense, decadence permitted the indulgence of popular entertainment in disregard of the class-delineated distinctions that existed across the landscape of London's cultural attractions at that time. Decadence did not see the role of art as elevation; rather, it saw it as a means of exploration. Many of the urban sights this prompted were informed by the themes of discovery found in travel accounts and exotic tales of the 'dark' continents, and London soon spawned a whole host of spectacles that offered the sights, sounds and smells of the world on a nightly basis. By the 1890s the desire to own and order the world's cultures was replaced by the desire to flaunt about in their robes and to recreate their rituals in the bid to demonstrate the aesthetic.

'Chrysanthemum Show at the Westminster Aquarium', late 1870s.

London was adept at staging effects drawn from the wealth of its empire, and the tattooed body was a common feature.

The Royal Aquarium in Westminster was typical of the pleasure palaces of the West End that offered all manner of worldly distractions, as the tattooist George Burchett recalled:

the dancing Zulu troupes, the swimming ladies from the South Seas and, above all the Zazelm 'Eighth wonder of the World'. He was shot out of a mammoth cannon three times nightly. Then there were some 'human oddities': dwarfs, bearded ladies and last, but not least, 'tattooed savages'.[4]

Many of these pleasure palaces blurred the distinction between spectator and spectacle by the participatory nature of their offerings. The Turkish bath and tattoo parlour on Jermyn Street operated in similar terms, distinguished only by the location and the associated charge of exclusivity.

Lynda Nead has recently traced a mythical rendering of London in this period as a Victorian Babylon, a vision that haunted urban renewal and modes of leisure by a fear of retribution from indulgence in excess.[5] This vision was a product of the artistic turn from the moralistic and narrative to the sensory and aesthetic over the course of the mid- to late nineteenth century. The tattooed body can therefore be seen as a daring indicator of this shift, marking immoral excess as a filigreed form of seepage across the whiteness of a London soul.

David W. Purdy is considered to be the first professional tattooer in nineteenth-century London, practising in the early 1870s from a booth in Holloway, not far from the prison. His pamphlet *Tattooing: How to Tattoo, What To Use and How To Use Them*, published in 1896, was his commercial response to an interest in tattooing that had expanded beyond his usual lowly clientele and beyond the 'pricking-in' of mere spots. Much of this can be garnered from the range of designs he offered, which included:

> the Tower Bridge, for instance, or the Great Wheel, at Earl's Court or the Imperial Institute, or one of Her Majesty's Battleships, and the Houses of Parliament, all making good pictures, which could be easily printed neatly on flesh; but never attempt to Tattoo yourself, as it is impossible, and you would only make a mess of it.

Although many of the designs would have been attractive to soldiers and sailors, the kinds of London landmarks suggested by Purdy indicate that they would also have been suitable for civilians interested in a permanent bit of patriotism. Purdy's guide is clear to point out, though, that the design and execution were always to be directed by the hand of a professional. The proximity of his business to the prison was to ensure him regular trade, but it also mapped a very explicit link between criminal bodies and tattoo designs that remained an issue for the appeal of the craft beyond this audience. The elevation of tattooing to an 'art' in the capital was achieved by Sutherland Macdonald and his competitors Tom Riley and Alfred South, who understood that this lay in changing the location.

Sutherland Macdonald is recognized for the exotic influences he brought to bear on his craft in an attempt to ennoble it from the lowly conception of tattooing. Described as a gentleman 'who had the manner and bearing of a Harley Street surgeon and the talent of a great painter',[6] he opened his studio underneath the Hammam Turkish bath of Jermyn Street, the street of men's outfitters equidistant from the shopping arcades of Mayfair and the gentleman's clubs of Pall Mall. Whilst serving in the Royal Engineers, Macdonald had learnt at close quarters the coarse art of tattooing amongst service men and he built upon this limited repertoire by observing the craft of Japanese tattooing, in particular the work of Hori Chyo, the celebrated tattoo artist who had tattooed the Duke of Clarence and the Duke of York (later George v). Macdonald not only learned Japanese techniques but also expanded upon them by devising non-traditional colours and designs of his own hand. In addition, the decoration of his studio was purposefully set out to imitate that of Hori Chyo's:

> A visit to the little studio at 'The Hammam' in Jermyn Street, is, in its way, as interesting as a visit to Chyo's bungalow, and whilst recognizing such salient features in both as the luxurious cushions, resting here on a divan instead of the floor, the familiar needles with their gaily decorated handles and the little hypodermic syringe, not to mention the ever-ready box of cigarettes and the accompanying cooling drinks, we find here the additional comforts of the electric light and a snug stove, both of them very necessary in the variable English climate. And quite as much time can be spent going through the portfolios of both, for whilst in those of Chyo's we find scarcely anything but the art of Japan, very beautiful and fascinating in its soft colouring and

dainty effects, in Macdonald's albums we find drawings and paintings gathered from all quarters of the globe, and of all and every kind, quaint, humorous and pathetic, but each one specially selected for the purpose of being reproduced by the tattooing-needles, and in more than one instance, the copyright of some particularly striking picture has actually been purchased outright, so that no one but the wealthier patrons of the Jermyn Street studio shall have the use of them.[7]

The re-creation of the interior of the Japanese bungalow was in keeping with the popularity of the Japanese village built in South Kensington in the early 1890s (which was central to Gilbert and Sullivan's creation of *The Mikado*), but it also contextualized the consumption of Macdonald's craft with the fashionable consumption of Japanese craft ware. This included blue and white porcelain ware collected as an artistic form of interior decoration in London by the likes of James McNeill Whistler and other aesthetes. They would often be complemented by woodblock prints that presented views of Japanese life, often featuring the floating world of pleasure districts where tattoo parlours were a common feature.

These tokens of Japanese culture were consumed in London not only for their voguishness, but also for their ability to propose an alternative model for living and a challenge to Western ideals of beauty. William Michael Rossetti published in 1863 an article in *The Reader* that praised Japanese woodcuts in illustrated books: 'Notwithstanding their grandeur and finesse of line, there is nothing in them which can be identified by a European as a feeling for beauty.'[8] The appreciation of these graphic woodcuts was soon transferred to an interest in the quality of line also found in tattoos. *The Strand* magazine's article on tattooing asserts this synthesis, albeit in terms that its readership would understand:

> The Japanese tattooers are celebrated all over the world, and in that country, at least, the work of the best men is recognised by their countrymen at a glance, and is looked upon with the awe and respect that we should show to a *chef d'œuvre* by Leighton or Tadema.[9]

Even though an imperial decree banning the practice of tattooing on Japanese people was enforced in Japan at this time, the craft survived by being practised in other countries on other bodies. But it was not the admiration that many Englishmen had for the craft that ensured its survival, but because it rejected the Victorian principle of moral beauty through the display of exoticism.

Looking through Sutherland Macdonald's book of designs one could easily appreciate that just as a dragon could unfurl down a back, so a serpent could entwine a wrist,

> whilst on the other hand a life-sized fly was put on an Englishman's wrist so naturally that one would be tempted to call his attention to the fact that the fly was getting a free lunch out of him, were we not told of the fact that it was the work of the tattooing needles.[10]

By setting his parlour below a Turkish bath Macdonald realized that the two businesses could coexist as an acceptable forum for the baring of bodies and the display of exotic tattoos in late Victorian London. The setting of a Japanese parlour below a Turkish bath underlines that, although culturally distinct in the experiences they offered, to the male frequenter of Jermyn Street their close combination was due to them both being purveyors of the exotic and the pleasurable.

The Hammam of Jermyn Street that Sutherland traded from had been opened in 1862 by the London & Provincial Turkish Bath Co. Ltd, a company owned by the Scottish diplomat David Urquhart and his associates from the Foreign Affairs Committee. When posted in Turkey in the 1850s, Urquhart wrote a narrative of his travels, *The Pillars of Hercules* (1848), which celebrated the architecture and experience of a Turkish bath. It cast a blueprint for the building and servicing of a range of Turkish baths built in Ireland and Britain. As his introduction modestly stated:

> I have no expectation that my suggestions will modify the lapel of a coat, or the leavening of a loaf; but there is one subject in which I am not without hope of having placed a profitable habit

more within the chance of adoption than it has hitherto been – I
mean the bath. Cleanliness, like inebriety or intemperance, may
be at once a fashion and a passion.[11]

Urquhart's intention was to set the charm of the Turkish bath between
the whim of fashion and the necessity of sustenance. The fame of the
Jermyn Street Hammam was further cemented by the novelist Anthony
Trollope in 1869. He utilized the environment of steam and towelled
clothing as the foil for the short story 'The Turkish Bath', concerning
mistaken identity. The story illuminates the levelling aspect of this
establishment, where a man seen to be sporting tattered gloves by two
literary editors on the street becomes, in the disguise of the steam room,
a cosmopolitan man who impresses his worldliness and charm upon the
same two men. (Much later Neil Bartlett made it the place where Mr
Clive encounters Mr Page in the 1950s, in his novel of 1996 entitled *Mr
Clive and Mr Page*.)

For the very reason that steam is not dissimilar to fog, I would argue
that the vapour of the Turkish bath can be convincingly tied to the
modernity of the London metropolis. The preoccupation with the poetical qualities of fog, mist and twilight as a way of reconfiguring and
abstracting the city became a crucial theme for many aesthetes and decadents in the late nineteenth century. For example, Whistler's *Nocturnes*
were views of the Thames at dusk that attempted in their titles a synthesis with the notation of music (he even painted a version of a *Nocturne*, a
view of the Thames and Battersea Bridge on a Japanese screen in 1872).
All were concerned with the eradication of a subject's precise outline in
order to invite contemplation by the imagination. Oscar Wilde was to
popularize this indeterminacy by declaring: 'At present, people see fogs,
not because there are fogs, but because poets and painters have taught
them the mysterious loveliness of such effects.'[12]

The attractiveness of fogs to the decadents was in their unfixed
nature, in how they cloaked the rationality of the city in visual terms. As
such, it gaily traded upon an earlier fear in London of a vapour that
assumed a kind of moral miasma. The medical principle of miasma,
popular in the mid-nineteenth century, was that disease was carried

James Abbott McNeill Whistler, *Nocturne in Blue and Silver: Cremorne Lights*, 1872, oil on canvas.

merely by the inhalation of noxious smells found in the city. It soon developed a moral dimension where it was believed that merely coming into contact with depraved areas of the city was enough to induce contagion with degeneracy. Though many took delight in this depraved vision of London smoking with noxious impulses, the true interest in poetic indeterminacy for the decadents lay not on the Thames at dusk, but in the rising heat of Babylonian places.

The conjuring of atmosphere from exotic trappings was to be found in J. K. Huysmans's novel *A rebours* (1884), which was to be fundamental to the aesthetic quality of *The Yellow Book,* an illustrated quaterly first published in 1894. This featured an interior colour scheme developed by the protagonist to be viewed only in subdued artificial lighting by night. The referencing of Gustave Moreau's painting of *Salome Dancing before Herod (Tattooed Salome)* of 1876 in the same fictional scheme was to be a direct influence on Wilde's decision to dramatize the biblical story

Gustave Moreau,
Salomé Dancing,
1876, oil on canvas.

and for Aubrey Beardsley to create the now notorious artwork for the poster. All were drawn to the rendering of Salome as a figure bejewelled and tattooed, accoutrements on alabaster skin set against a richly coloured setting evoking heat and musk. (There was even a tattooed lady of the time known as Salome who toured Europe.)

The Middle East had long been the setting for the exoticism of romantic literature, and with the colonial expansion of trade topographical paintings and portraits of Europeans in Middle Eastern fancy dress became popular. More specifically, the Middle Eastern interior as a site of speculation and mystery was prevalent in depictions of the palace, the harem and the Turkish bath where light filtered through filigreed screens and heat is subdued by decorative stonework. The centrality of the *femme fatale* in these scenes, not naked but decorated, was another trope that haunted late nineteenth-century literature, painting and even architecture. The best surviving example of this kind of interior in London is Leighton House, the Kensington home and studio of the society artist Lord Leighton.

The icon of the *femme fatale*, and especially Salome, was attractive to the many women who were beginning to achieve greater independence. A popular tattoo design for women was the eternal serpent as a bracelet around the wrist or a necklace around the neck that referenced the role of Eve and the snake in man's expulsion from the Garden of Earthly Delight. Lady Randolph Churchill, Sir Winston Churchill's mother, had an eternal serpent bracelet tattoo applied by Tom Riley in London. Interviewed for the *Pall Mall Gazette* in 1889, the tattooist Sutherland Macdonald confirmed that women formed a section of his clientele:

> 'Of what class are the majority of your customers then?' – 'Mostly officers in the army, but civilians too. I have tattooed many noblemen, and also several ladies. The latter go in chiefly for ornamentation on the wrist or calf, or have a garter worked on just below the knee. One lady came to me to have a beauty spot marked on her face, but I should not be surprised to see her back some day with a request that I should eradicate it.'[13]

This is further confirmed by an article in *Tatler* magazine in 1903, which reported that Alfred South of Cockspur Street had tattooed more than 900 women:

> There are some instances where ladies have had the inscriptions on their wedding rings tattooed on their fingers beneath the ring. Ladies who like to keep pace with the times may be adorned with the illustration of motorcars.[14]

These articles confirm that considerable numbers of women were tattooed in London at the time and that the designs they requested were as esoteric as those asked for by men. As we will see later, tattooing moved into the area of permanent make-up for women with the advent of the cosmetics industry in the 1930s, but at this point a tattooed metropolitan women still ran the risk of being thought of as a side-show attraction.

The travelling exhibition of heavily tattooed men and women was a popular feature of late Victorian London. Here, it was traditionally the wife of the tattoo artist who bore most of her husband's designs, acting as a human canvas to aid the securing of commissions and the fame of her husband's hand. The most common designs were the accoutrements of dress tattooed directly onto the relevant part of the body, such as knee-high laced boots or necklaces. To protect their modesty, the women would often wear tight-fitting black costumes, a very basic kind of body stocking to cover the other areas of their body. As the number of tattoos increased, so too did these women's visibility as prized wonders of the travelling world, with their fame often circulated through the selling of *cartes de visites*. These women were marginalized from mainstream society, but conversely they appreciated in symbolic value as decorative forms that artists and in turn certain women found aspirational in their ability visually to flaunt convention and conformity.

The women tattooed by Mr Macdonald, Mr Riley and Mr South differ in that they were not married to a tattoo artist and they did not become a sideshow attraction. In the concealed nature of their designs, hidden behind a wedding ring or posing as a bracelet set behind a cuff, they offered these women a badge of difference that was hidden from a moral society that would not allow them to bare their skins in public – not even in a Turkish bath.

In her book *Bodies of Subversion: Women and Tattoos*, Margot Mifflin claims that Edward Burne-Jones and other artists of the Pre-Raphaelite Brotherhood were particularly entranced by the idea of the fully decorated female form and would often frequent sideshow spectacles to gain the friendship of such women, who were not averse to baring their skins. The aesthetic writer Algernon Swinburne, who was the first to review Charles Baudelaire's *Les Fleurs du mal* (1857) in English, a book that was subsequently to inform decadence, was famous for courting an American circus performer. Such liaisons were key examples of the modernist style of mixing the high with the low.

The American tattooed lady Emma de Burgh toured Europe in the 1890s, bearing a reproduction of Leonardo da Vinci's *Last Supper* across her shoulder blades and the American Eagle and the Union Jack on each kneecap. After seeing her, Burne-Jones wrote that fame had made her visibly complacent: 'she had grown very stout . . . and when I looked at the Last Supper all the apostles wore broad grins'.[15] Similarly, John Dixon Hunt once claimed that by the 1890s the Pre-Raphaelite ideal of female beauty was one of hackneyed decoration inscribed over an ideal of beauty, not unlike a tattooed lady in decline. This change can also be traced through the programming of attractions at the Royal Aquarium, where Burne-Jones may well have seen de Burgh because it was close to his home in Chelsea.

In his memoirs, the tattooist George Burchett describes how he began his career in the 1870s as a billiards marker at the newly opened Aquarium. He progressed to tattooing after befriending the tattooed ladies who worked there, most of whom were not actually that exotic, having been 'born within the sound of Bow bells'. The Westminster Aquarium (also known as the Royal Aquarium and Summer and Winter Garden) was opened in 1876 by the Prince of Wales as a place of entertaining education, but it quickly fell into disrepute because of a lack of investment and poor management. From the initial offerings of a large aquarium of fish and an exhibition of paintings by Millais, the attractions soon descended into dangerous and risqué spectacles that forced its licence to be revoked on many occasions. These included Captain George Costentenus, a tattooed man who was the central attraction in 1882, bearing 'the prolonged and horrible agony of this combination of Barbaric Art and Vengeance necessitated over 7,000,000 Punctures of the Quivering Flesh', while 'combining in one exhibition a picture gallery'.[16]

The shift in the Aquarium's attractions, from a fixed exhibition of paintings to a living exhibition of tattoos, demonstrates the parallel move from cultured education to salacious entertainment in the

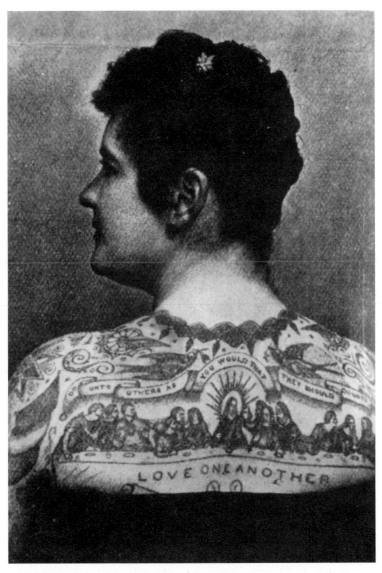

Emma de Burgh with Leonardo's *Last Supper* tattooed on her back, date unknown.

Variety of late Victorian London. It marks the transfer of the female form as an ideal of beauty, education and reform into one of exoticism, entertainment and speculation. The presence of tattooing is important in visibly marking the shift from a figure 'painted' according to artistic ideals to a figure 'inscripted' by some sense of its own ideals.

This is confirmed in two consecutive pages from an early book of George Burchett's tattoo designs from the early part of the twentieth century. The first faithfully depicts a Japanese Geisha girl in traditional dress, the second a Variety girl in stage costume. While the former was thought of as an example of high culture in the period, the latter was castigated as a form of low culture, yet their sequential placing in the design book confirms the connections that the craft of tattooing was able to map across cultural distinctions and social bodies thought of as fashionable.

Two tattoo designs by George Burchett, early 1900s.

The peculiar kinds of designs that this short-lived fashion prompted can be thought of as maps of the decadent imagination that mark the tattooed body as peculiarly modern. As flights of fancy eternally engraved on the skin they covertly challenged the prevailing moral codes of the day.

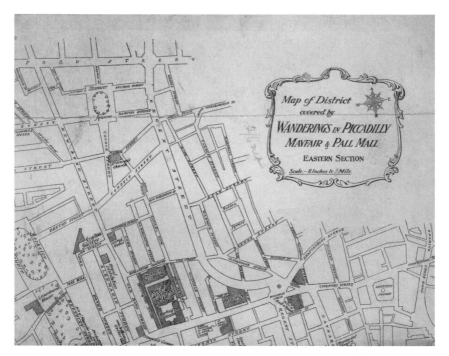

Detail of map from E. Beresford Chancellor, *Wanderings in Piccadilly, Mayfair & Pall Mall* (1908).

CHAPTER TWO

In a map reproduced at the front of Beresford Chancellor's guide of 1908, Wanderings in Piccadilly, Mayfair and Pall Mall, *one can see that the distance between our first site of enquiry on Jermyn Street and the next in Hanover Square is not far. (If one were able to walk directly through Burlington House, the home of the Royal Academy of Arts, it could be achieved in a straight line; and according to the scale of the map, the distance is less than half a mile.) But before dealing with the exploits of early British couture that traded under the name of Lucile, I want to draw attention to a poster printed by the Westminster Aquarium before its demise that caused an inordinate amount of controversy.*

It features Zaeo the acrobat, and moral campaigners were enraged at the representation of her skimpy costume and the sight line that the male audience is given of her performing on an aerial rope. A Mr Coote of the National Vigilance Society claimed that 'Londoners must be led to the conviction that this lady actually appeared in the same nude condition'. Although Zaeo did not appear naked, she was promoted and presented through the illusion of being so. It is a spectacular vision of a woman, and this kind of image proved to be influential in the way in which fashionable dress for women was promoted at the beginning of the twentieth century in London. Today, Hanover Square is well known as the address for Vogue House, the place where the monthly definition of a British woman in Vogue *is made. But I want to consider a definition of a fashionable woman made in Hanover Square in an age before the advent of British* Vogue.

WEBB POPPLETON LOW   FLAMING WILLIAM DISSENT.   HUGH GOOD-CHAP BROAD

ZÆO TRIUMPHANT.

'Zæo Triumphant', poster for the Aquarium, from a supplement to *The Music Hall and Theatre Review*, 16 August 1890.

Chancellor noted in his guide that what had once been a charming London square was now almost entirely at the service of commerce. Hanover Square

> has almost entirely lost that residential character with which it began its fashionable career, there luckily survive some of the original houses – nos 17 & 18 being cases in point . . . Today in these are found clubs, fashionable dressmakers, learned societies, anything you will except private residences.[1]

What Chancellor failed to note was that many of these businesses favoured properties in Hanover Square precisely because it offered the air of a private residence. Until only recently no. 17 had been occupied by Mrs Jordan, an actress who had gained notoriety for being favoured by the Duke of Clarence (also tattooed by Sutherland McDonald), before in 1897 becoming the commercial premises of Lady Duff Gordon, who traded under the name of Lucile. From the day it opened, Lucile traded dressmaking from an address already steeped in the romantic convergence of English Society and London theatre. As such, it was the first step in the professionalization of the marketing and presentation of high-end fashion produced in London.

The earliest professional fashion models are thought to have emerged at the same time, around the beginning of the twentieth century. The attire that identified them was a black silk undergarment not unlike those devised by the wives of tattoo artists or performing acrobats. In presenting their bodies to a moral public, they all had to retain a modicum of decency and refrain from appearing naked, even though they might actually be clothed. The shapes and cuts demanded were yet to be catered for in the ready-made market, so female performers often resorted to making their own outfits that looked not unlike modern-day negligee, but would often be made from a rigid black silk or satin. Employers provided similar garments for their fashion models; these generally included full-length sleeves, so as not to expose anything in the way of unwanted flesh.

17, HANOVER SQUARE
my first big venture, where I started "Mannequin" Parades

Maison Lucile: '17 Hanover Square, my first big venture, where I started "Mannequin" Parades', from the memoirs of Lady Duff Gordon ('Lucile'), *Discretions and Indiscretions* (1932).

The high-end dress designer Lucile, based in Hanover Square, was the first in London to abandon the practice of models wearing undergarments for her fashion presentations. For this she was accused of peddling a 'cult of immoral dressing', and some thought it was more indecent than a side-show of a woman bearing her decorated flesh. Yet even though Lucile's clothes were often in the fleshiest of tones, her clients always remained fully clothed. To achieve this, she employed techniques drawn from the theatrical variety stages of the West End and the salacious presentation of Living Pictures, which were tableaux of women in tight-fitting, flesh-coloured, silk body stockings mimicking famous nudes painted by old masters (the trick being that they appeared naked when under the stage lights). Like the tattooed lady, this ideal of femininity was also an artistic one, but one that reflects a shift from the adoration of the female form as exotic decoration to its illusory presentation as an artistic depiction.

These glamorous projections remained crucial to the promotion of fashionable ideals for women across the first span of the twentieth century. This is an account of how a fashion designer learnt from the stage and applied its principles to high-end clothing designs: by abandoning the black outfits worn by models and performers for modesty and investing in the trickery of nude-coloured outfits for their visual and permissive suggestion of immorality.

By the turn of the twentieth century, the fashion for all things decadent had been scorched by the dawn of the new age. The pace of invention accelerated the speeding of modern life in London; electricity fostered faster transportation and communication technologies, travelling wavelengths of sound and the deft flicker of the moving image. The increased pace of life in London at this point and the newly developed sights and sounds it offered meant that, for many people, a visit to the West End was to encounter a barrage of sensations, where the fashion for change was experienced as a kind of velocity. Early filmic depictions of London life give an eerie demonstration of this idea: the jilting and flickering images show crowds moving through the city at a pace that is obviously not their own.

If decadence was no longer in fashion, then what replaced it was another artistic mode of consumption, but one that was framed by the fusing of femininity and commodity culture as a form of visual enticement. Walter Benjamin, who believed that the commodity tinged the sex appeal of all modern women, first established this relationship between the presentation of women and the allure of the modern commodity as a kind of fetishism.

The idea of a woman on display was nothing new, but the interrelationships between the new kinds of spaces in which she could be found mapped a new identity. These artistic visions of femininity presented on theatrical stages and those built in fashion salons built a web of connections hitherto unseen, illuminating them as informed by the associations of light and electricity as symbolic sources of power and modernity. These staged presentations also served as alluring advertisements for the fashionable consumption of theatrically inspired dress designs.

In the West End of London, electric lighting was first noticeably installed in the newly built theatres, illuminating the stage, stalls and façades of these pleasure palaces. The brightness of these attractions and the way in which things sparkled when under the illuminations were to have a direct influence on the design and marketing of high-end dressmaking (or what could be considered early couture), particularly in Hanover Square, to the south of Oxford Street and the side of Regent Street, under the direction of Lady Duff Gordon and her business, Lucile. In *The Glass of Fashion*, Cecil Beaton recalled some of the costumes that he had witnessed as a child on the London stage designed by Lucile:

> The leading lady's gowns were inevitably made by Lucile and were masterpieces of intricate workmanship. It was the fashion for women to wear high-wasted Directoire dresses, falling straight to the floor, where the wearer's feet would be encumbered by bead-fringes and possibly clinging trains. Lucile worked with soft materials, delicately sprinkling them with bead or sequin embroidery, with cobweb lace insertions, true lovers' knots, and garlands of minute roses. Her colour sense was so subtle that the delicacy of detail could scarcely be seen at a distance, though the effect she created was an indefinable shimmer.[2]

This 'indefinable shimmer' characterizes the particular kind of glamour borne by Lucile's dress designs. It was a glamour that flickered and radiated as if illuminated by electrical light, whether on the stage or projected elsewhere. It was the ways in which the many trimmings of a dress caught the light and reflected it back in a myriad of sparkles that gave the wearer an aura of individuality. Lucile's experiments as both a fashion and a theatre costume designer were in an age before the relationship between fashion, the cinema and consumption was cemented by American Hollywood. However, her acute understanding of how to market her dress designs on the theatrical stage and on the stage she built in her salon marks her as an important figure in the genesis of the fashion show and the idea of a woman presented as a flickering image.

'A "Mannequin" Parade in 1913 in the garden at Lucile's, 23 Hanover Square', from *Discretions and Indiscretions*.

In her autobiography of 1932, *Discretions and Indiscretions*, Lucile credited herself with the invention of the first fashion salon presentation and the abandoning of the black silk bodices that models wore under their clothes for the purposes of modesty. While the originality of her fashion shows may now be discredited (Charles Frederick Worth in Paris is now considered an earlier precedent), the relationship of her presentations to stage costume design is more consistent than the likes of her better known French contemporary Paul Poiret. In a letter of 1928 written by Lady Duff Gordon to the Museum of London offering two early examples of her dress designs made for the London stage favourites Miss Lily Elsie and Miss Gertie Millar, the designer made claims to the importance of the dresses in the hope that the museum might acquire them:

> They were also part of a mannequin show with which I opened the Paris branch of Lucile Limited (1910) – an occasion when an English designer working with English work people caused something of a sensation by presenting the dresses on lovely English

model girls with suitable gloves, shoes, jewels, etc. to complete the costume, whereas until that time the French dressmakers had always shown their dresses on mannequins wearing long sleeved black satin slips, giving the exact appearance of dummies.[3]

In her letter Duff Gordon crystallizes the potent combination that made her such a stir in London, Paris and even New York: theatrical dress parading as fashion, working-class girls transformed Pygmalion-like into fashion models, and the abandoning of undergarments in favour of a visual idea of flesh. It was a heady cocktail that stirred erotic connotations into the presentation of fashion, so that the prospect of witnessing 'the glow of youthful flesh, or the curve of young ankles' became an object of pilgrimage and pleasure for men and women alike.[4]

Lucile's first commission as a theatre costume designer was for a production of *The Liars* at the Criterion Theatre in 1897. A review described it

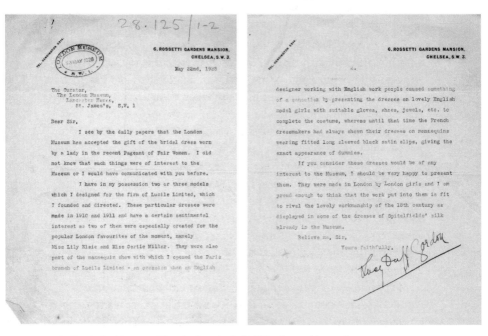

Letter to the Museum of London from Lady Duff Gordon, 22 May 1928.

as 'the bleakest of the decade's comedies of modern life, the rot beneath its glittering surface'. This was, of course, a reference to the spectacular costume designs featured, but it suggests that the glittering foil conceals all that is rotten about modern living, as the play suggests. This combination supports the idea suggested by many historians that the feminine figure is an equivalent to the attraction and repulsion of modernity in this period. *The Liars* was a stage play that fitted the trend of the 1890s for fashion plays and musical comedies featuring the latest dress designs available in the capital. The stages of the West End appeared to women as a series of shop windows that offered fashion-plate dramas.

Fashion designers and theatre managers had realized that they had similar spaces of exhibition and display and they quickly welcomed the economic prospect of collusion between the two. The spectacular visions that this union brought 'veiled the commercial nature of the transaction in theatrical illusion', according to Caroline Evans. The oscillation between the theatrical and the fashionable was also a flickering that was neither one nor the other, but fantastically the two.

Further, in the confusion between the appropriate site for the staging of the transaction, consumption and entertainment became intertwined. Shopping for clothes at this high end of the market posed as a dramatic re-fashioning of the self, with the theatrical presentation posing as a demonstration that could be re-enacted elsewhere. Identifications between audience and shopper, model and actress, abounded further.

Lucile remains one of the earliest examples of a designer selecting and training her own fashion models. At this point, modelling was still a lowly profession (it was not until after World War One that it was ennobled through the emergence of fashion photography in magazine publishing), so Lucile recruited working-class girls whom she trained in deportment and then renamed as exotic creatures drawn from mysterious climes. With names such as Gamela and Hebe, these young women became the living embodiment of a Lucile customer and what she should wear. However, it remained unlikely that an affluent patron would wish to look like a working-class girl transformed Pygmalion-like into a figure of exoticism.

Lucile overcame this obstacle by trading upon the idea that the transformative roles that can be played upon the stage by an actress are aided by the notion of character implicit in stage costume. In transferring this idea to the fashion presentations she staged in her salon, she was able to project the suspension of disbelief necessary to make a society lady want to dress like a working girl. Peter Bailey has written that in the first fifteen years of the twentieth century there was a 'glamourisation' of women in the capital. The role of actresses, chorus girls, working girls in the needle trades and service sectors, such as the department store, brought visible difference to the sexual landscape of the streets of London. The glamour they brought was very much conditioned and controlled by the contexts in which they were found working; but at this point dress began to play a role in veiling the zoning of these environments and the kind of women found in them – the difference, say, between being on stage, or in the stalls; waiting at the sales counter, or serving behind it.

The possibilities of dress offered a discreet form of subterfuge from the rigid definitions of identity for women bound by class and status. This transformative quality of dress permitted a certain respite from the constrictive roles demanded of women at this time, a camouflage of stealth, a trick of the eye that permitted an imaginative sense of movement across social strata, schemas of work, even socializing spaces. In this period dress for women working in the metropolis became a technology of the self, a form of self-improvement that was largely undefined by dress reform, modesty or propriety. It was a technology of the self fed by the technologies of design and production and circuited between the salon and the stage. The effect was chiefly in being seen as dressed to play a part.

Lucile achieved this illusion by coining her clothes 'Gowns of Emotion', also referred to at the time as personality dresses. She used it to promote the idea that the clothes she made in her early career were individual to each client. As a working practice, this went somewhat against the model of practice for a couturier established by Worth, who always decided the blueprint for what his clients could wear; Lucile's approach suggested that the inspiration of what could be termed fashionable was drawn from the innate quality of each of her clients individually: a dress that could suit their personality rather than their needs.

As her business expanded, it soon became impossible to name every dress individually, so the practice soon started to evidence a stock set of emotions that could be purchased. As such, it was in keeping with the modern malaise of emotions being read on the exterior surface of the body rather than emanating from the interior, fed by the speeding of metropolitan life and ever-condensing living conditions. The disassociation between the actual status of the working-class girls and the projected status driven by the clothes they modelled supported this discrepancy even further.

Lucile's 'Gowns of Emotions' were given titles such as 'The Captain's Whiskers', 'The Sighing Sound of Lips Unsatisfied' and 'Twilight and Memories'. In turning the pages of a surviving pattern book from 1905 housed at the Victoria and Albert Museum, one is unable to resist constructing one's own narrative for the titles that caption the dress design documented on each page: 'Unforgotten', 'Enrapture', 'The Moment', 'Oblivion', 'Afterwards – Nothing'. In associating the appearance of a dress with an 'inner' state of mind, the provocative titles are prosaic epitaphs to the moment when the status of dress in society extended beyond social hierarchy and towards signifying a psychological state. Gilles Lipovetsky underlined this when he wrote: 'Haute couture unleashed an original process within the fashion order: it psychologized fashion by creating designs that gave concrete form to emotions, personality, and character traits.'[5]

What is also particular about Lucile's titles is their strict similarity to the themes of love found in the fashionable and salacious novels written by her sister, Elinor Glyn, who wore her sister's designs, interweaving literary as well as psychological themes around these titles. Many of Glyn's novels featured well-dressed women with descriptions that faithfully ape the designs of Maison Lucile; further, Glyn's most successful novel, *Three Weeks* (1907), was a piece of semi-autobiographical fiction concerning a woman who has an affair with a younger man. (She later attempted to play the part herself in a stage adaptation, but the financier pulled out.) The following passage from *Three Weeks* fuses heroine, dress design, the pursuit of reading and the interior scheme as *mise-en-scène*:

> A bright fire burnt in the grate and some palest orchid-mauve silk curtains were drawn in the lady's room . . . in front of the fire, stretched at full length, was his tiger – and on him – also at full length reclined the lady, garbed in some strange clinging garment of heavy purple crepe, its hem embroidered with gold, one white arm resting on the beast's head, her back supported by a pile of the velvet cushions, and a heap of rarely bound books at her side, while between her red lips was a rose not redder than they – an almost scarlet rose . . . the whole picture was barbaric.[6]

The fame of the 'picture' that became exchangeable in the popular consciousness with the popularity of the novel bestowed upon the author the following ditty, which would have been familiar to many a Londoner:

> Would you like to sin
> With Elinor Glyn
> On a tiger-skin?
> Or would you prefer
> To err
> With her
> On some other fur?[7]

The novel was eventually made into a silent film. A crucial feature of Glyn's literary style was to describe the dress of her heroines as if perpetually 'shimmering' and 'gleaming' with 'brilliancy'. Although this is a literary technique deployed to indicate the aura of the protagonist, it closely relates to historical descriptions of Lucile's fashion and stage designs, lending further credence to the centrality of the shimmer to an understanding of the designer's career.

The expanded potential of mass-produced clothing in this period facilitated not uniformity, but the means by which individuality,

A poster for Alan Crossland's 1924 film of Elinor Glyn's novel *Three Weeks*, in which the actress famously reclines on a tiger skin.

expressed by the many nuances of clothing, could flourish. However, most of the innovations were realized in the pursuit of imitating the materials of hand-crafted objects of desire made by hand-crafted means: machined lace looking as if crocheted by hand, industrially glazed cotton looking like taffeta. The fashion for such specialized fabrics and trimmings for female dress was not new, yet the heightened manner in which Lucile as a designer was to use these materials for her designs – mixing the ostentatious with the gaudy, the luxurious with the machine-made – was to draw attention to the ability of these things to sparkle: effervescent from the wonder of technological potential when applied to spectacular dress in abundance. Duff Gordon confirms this in her autobiography:

> For me there was a positive intoxication in taking yards of shimmering silks, laces airy as gossamer and lengths of ribbons, delicate and rainbow-coloured, and fashioning them of garments, so lovely that they might have been worn by some princess in a fairy tale.[8]

While in time Coco Chanel was to believe the modernist principle that you should start with the dress rather than the trimmings, Duff Gordon believed that early twentieth-century modernity was to be found in the cornucopia of materials to which she could lay her hand and the effects she could produce with them en masse. Her designs reflected the expanded production and consumption of women's fashions within this period, observed from the isolated but influential perspective of high-end dress design for a limited and London-based clientele.

Recently divorced from an alcoholic husband, with little formal education and no income bar a small inheritance from her recently deceased father, in 1889 Lucy persuaded her mother to back her financially as a dressmaker, capitalizing on her only practical skill of sewing. Even though she would have been thought *déclassé* for plying a trade for a living, it was in the act of selling her wares, in her role as a *vendeuse* to society ladies, that ennobled her position.

Her first design was based on a tea gown inspired by a dress worn by an actress on stage, and it became her first calling card for society ladies, worn by The Hon. Mrs Arthur Brand on the occasion of her staying with a society hostess. The loose and uncorseted style of the garment implied if not a state of undress then at least a private and introspective state on the part of the wearer. Duff Gordon seized on the risqué potential of the tea gown as a way of challenging late Victorian London's views on modesty and morality in women's dress, whilst championing her own cause for notoriety.

The association of the tea gown with refreshment and sociability among women became actively embedded in the business that Lucile ran, most notably at her second Hanover Square salon (no. 17 opened in 1897, no. 23 in 1901). Her belief that 'nobody had thought of developing the social side of choosing clothes, of serving tea and imitating the setting of a drawing-room' nurtured her idea that a commercial space for the selling of clothing could appear as a space of leisure and domesticity.[9] A commemorative photograph of the first dress worn by her first client hung on the walls of each of her establishments, which expanded to include outlets in Paris (established in 1910) and New York (opened in 1912).

The second showroom on Hanover Square was the most celebrated decorative scheme of all. Set into a well-proportioned Adam room with an Angelica Kauffmann ceiling, the scheme was based on an eighteenth-century concept of decorative restraint: shades of painted grey, matching silk taffeta curtains and silk-covered Louis XV gilt chairs. The interior design was to act as a neutral foil to the more overworked dress designs, and it bore influence on the taste of the decorator Elsie de Wolfe, who was a friend of Duff Gordon. To the side of the large ballroom lay a small anteroom that contained Lucile's range of underwear for women, lain on a day-bed ordered from Paris that was purportedly a replica of the one owned by Madame de Pompadour, hinting at the risqué idea that one could be both arbiter of taste and a kept woman.

The main feature of the ballroom was a small stage with a set of olive-green curtains, which formed the focus for the presentations, before the models descended and walked among the invited audience. This sense of observing fashion in motion (not quite on the theatre stage, not quite everyday reality) was novel to London at this time. A black dress from around 1910 in the Victoria and Albert Museum's collection reveals the designer's keen understanding of the purpose of movement to realize

Lucile fashion presentation, c. 1910, Hanover Square, from *Discretions and Indiscretions*.

Black silk chiffon evening dress perhaps associated with the actress Gertie Millar, made by Lucile, c. 1910, and donated to the Victoria and Albert Museum, London.

fully the potential of a dress design. The silk-lined black chiffon dress softly defines a cap-sleeved and fitted bodice before extending under the bust to a full skirt with short train. The fringes of jet beading at the train and falling from the Empire line are purposefully placed to move quite spectacularly when the figure encased in it is in motion; undoubtedly, the dress has a strong sense of dynamism about it.

We can appreciate that a woman dressed in such a gown, or in those described by Cecil Beaton, would look not unlike an actual illumination herself, as opulent in filigree as a glass-sharded chandelier, or in colours as richly hued as any hand-blown shade. It was at this time that West End theatres began to install electric rather than gas lighting to improve the brightness of their illuminations and the quality of the spectacle in a bid to out-dazzle the competition.

Interestingly, the newly created visual identities of the power companies that supplied the theatres with electrical illuminations bore similar visual tropes. In order to create trademarks for what were essentially intangible forms of power supply, the companies developed logos drawn from mythological and art-historical imagery for their ability to raise themes of beauty and transcendence. Unusually, the house of Lucile also drew from similar reference points, but those found in the electrically illuminated presentations of old master paintings on the stages of London's variety theatres.

In their re-creation of old master paintings for the purposes of 'education', Living Pictures, or Poses Plastiques as they were also known, were a fixture of the variety bill that presented women as if naked but in fact fully clothed in flesh-coloured body stockings. The lighting tricks and composure of the models necessary to make a maillot look like bare skin are likely to have been closely studied by Duff Gordon, who copied them for her own fashion presentations, creating a form of atmosphere that was intended as the illuminated embodiment of theatre and desire.

Society ladies such as Duff Gordon were introduced first-hand to the art of Living Pictures by those daring enough to play a part in their staging for the purpose of raising money for charity. Her sister, Elinor Glyn, took part in a charity matinee at Her Majesty's Theatre in 1900 to raise money for a South African War Charity organized by Lady Arthur Paget. Five red-headed ladies – Glyn, Mrs Curzon, Lady Mary Sackville, Baroness d'Erlanger and Lady St Oswald – recreated Titian's painting *The Five Senses* under the direction of Max Beerbohm Tree. The producer insisted that they put copper dust in their hair to enrich and unify their hair colours, which promptly turned their hair green under the heat of the stage lights.

The interest with which Duff Gordon took to this kind of 'art' is interesting in that it goes somewhat against the prevailing taste for the depiction of couture in paintings. Ed Lilley has suggested that with the rise of couture in the mid- to late nineteenth century the nude as a symbol of femininity painted by artists became eclipsed by the spectacularity of women's dress, which began to play a more active role in the representation of femininity in art.[10] This was a shift from the artist's model to a fashion model, from a model unclothed to one clothed. The inversion of this trend represented by Duff Gordon's costumes made to look like flesh is therefore an interesting anomaly.

As a spectacle of popular entertainment, *tableaux vivants* sought to reinvest old master paintings with their erotic potential by using live models dressed so as to appear naked. This was one result of variety producers' creative response to the rulings of the Lord Chamberlain's Office, which inspected the content of staged plays in London to check for offensiveness to royalty, indecency and blasphemy, and forbade any form of nudity on stage. In a review of a Living Pictures presentation at the Palace Theatre on Cambridge Circus in 1895, George Bernard Shaw, author of *Pygmalion*, noted:

> I need hardly say that the ladies who impersonated the figures in these pictures were not actually braving our climate without any protection . . . what was presented as flesh was really spun silk . . . the Living Pictures are not only works of art: they are excellent practical sermons; and I urge every father of a family who cannot afford to send his daughters the round of the picture galleries . . . to take them all (with their brothers) to the Palace Theatre.[11]

Loie Fuller as Salomé, from the Sixth Series of the Palace Tableaux Vivants, week of Monday, 2 December 1895, The Palace Theatre, London, from a review in *The Times*, 11 December 1895.

With just the right amount of irony Shaw mocked it as art history but embraced it as an education of quite another sort. These re-enactments cited the erotic not on the body, but on a fabric that imitated it on the surface of the skin. It was a form of eroticism that was displaced and impersonal – but reassuringly voyeuristic. Those who campaigned against such displays, staged largely at the Empire Theatre, Leicester Square, and the Palace Theatre at Cambridge Circus, were forced to decry them through the ungainliness of the costumes, often revealed through poor art direction or an unrehearsed movement. As a National

Vigilance Campaigner noted on seeing a Poses Plastiques of Ariadne by Johann Daunecher:

> Ariadne . . . so far as I can put it into language, represents a naked woman lying on the back of a lion. There were four or five wrinkles on the lower part of the limb, distinguishing it from an ordinary picture. The left leg was placed under the lower part of the right leg, producing these wrinkles. She was lying in such a position that had it not been for the tights gross indecency would have been the result.[12]

What was so repugnant to the moral campaigners was that a titillating and unstable form of eroticism could be objectified into material form: a second skin that could be put on, paraded and then taken off again, detaching desire and sexuality from the individual and constructing it into a costume solely for visual titillation. In the short-lived time that Living Pictures were all the rage at the Variety Theatre, *The Sketch* magazine noted that:

> It may be interesting to mention that the beautifully fitting tights in which all these lovely girls are encased are especially made of these tableaux by a London firm, even the fingers and toes having been carefully modelled, thus preventing any line which would be caused by the material ending at the ankle or wrist.[13]

I would ague that Lucile's personality dresses operated in similar terms, as a second skin that could be worn for a particular effect. Even her stage costumes received reviews that could easily have been mistaken for a Living Picture costume. A review for 'The Merry Widow' of 1907, one of her most celebrated costume designs, was described as 'what appears to be woven sunshine but is in reality a shimmer of silver and gold embroideries over oyster-white satin'.[14]

Lucile's first costumes for the stage, for the production of *The Liars* in 1897, were noted for being lighter in weight, more colourful, and more body-conscious than the norm, and were described as bearing a 'heightened naturalism'.[15] Her understanding of how costume moves on the body under the lights was to bear strong influence on her dress designs, so that what could well have been construed as indecent exposure was instead projected as a form of radiance. In the very same year the Empire Theatre was to show the first moving-picture film to be screened in Great Britain, eclipsing the attraction of its variety programme. While Elinor Glyn was eventually to establish herself as an author who successfully wrote for Hollywood films, Duff Gordon was unable to make the successful translation as a costume designer from stage to screen. Yet her ruminations on film costume from the sidelines demonstrate a curious relation to her own ideas about the sightliness of female flesh:

> Now the most important point in making dresses for the screen is that they must be so tight that there is not even an extra inch of material to cause unnecessary wrinkles, otherwise the fit of a beautiful dress can be ruined when it is seen through the camera. Hollywood has, therefore, formed the invariable habit of being fitted with nothing on underneath the dress.[16]

In abolishing the black satin undergarment from her fashion presentations and in her interest in flesh-coloured costumes for the stage, Duff Gordon was motivated towards similar effects, seeking to resurrect the erotic potential of women. The modernity of her endeavour was that she understood the mechanics of seeing things cinematically – from the sight level of an audience watching something in motion. She made dresses that flickered fluidly, that radiated a sexuality that was illuminated on the surface.

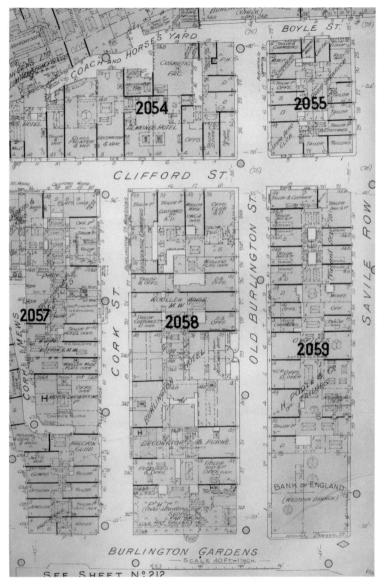

Fire Regulation Map showing part of Burlington Gardens (London ix), September 1928.

CHAPTER THREE

Lucile's dress designs had a profound impact on the artistic sensi-
bilities of the next generation, particularly for their lavish sense
of theatricality. The theatrical imagination and the world of
fashion strongly infused the British strain of Surrealism when it
arrived in London in the mid-1930s. The link between these two
ages is the figure of Miss Lily Elsie, famed for her role in The
Merry Widow *with her costumes designed by Lucile. She was*
the woman that Cecil Beaton first fell in love with at the tender
age of four, and the bride for whom the artist Eileen Agar should
have been bridesmaid. But over and above all this, it was her
large-brimmed 'Merry Widow' hat that would translate into the
1930s and play another starring, but quite different role.

Doubling back on the route from Jermyn Street to Hanover
Square just taken, walking south from Hanover Square past St
George's Church and across Conduit Street into an area of a few
short streets – one arrives at a point where the worlds of English
tailoring and British art converge.

Poster for the *International Surrealist Exhibition* at the New Burlington Galleries, London, 1936.

Surrealism descended on London on 11 June 1936. The occasion was the opening of the *International Surrealist* exhibition at the New Burlington Galleries at 5 Burlington Gardens, Mayfair; and the British press went wild. More than 2,000 guests attended the event to witness at first hand what Surrealism looked like and how its many artists behaved. On arrival, guests were greeted by the Welsh poet Dylan Thomas, who offered them teacups brim-full with cut string as refreshment, asking intermittently: 'Do you like it weak, or do you like it strong?' Then they would catch sight of André Breton, dressed in a green suit, and his wife, her long hair dyed pen-ink green. Visiting on later days, they may have caught sight of the British composer William Walton pinning a mackerel to an assemblage by Miró, or strained to hear Salvador Dalí's lecture on 'Paranoia', where he was flanked by two hounds and wore a deep-sea diving suit. His muffled proclamations about his love for his wife Gala continued until he was rescued from the suit, so near did he come to suffocation.

The heat of the opening night ensured that one of Dalí's exhibits, *Aphrodisiac Dinner Jacket* (1936), a gentleman's dinner jacket covered in glasses of crème de menthe, evaporated its alcoholic content. (Ruthven Todd, the assistant secretary, came up with the good idea of using green ink and water, perhaps inspired by Breton's wife's hair.) Those looking around for drinkable refreshment may only have caught sight of Meret Oppenheim's seminal artwork, *Le Déjeuner en fourrure* (1936), of a fur cup and saucer, exhibited in Britain for the first time.

Many of the reports in the popular press were unconcerned with how the artworks unsettled the conscious assumptions of the everyday, or their political implications (ridicule was much easier), but they were very much taken by the artists who had made them. By far the most striking was Sheila Legge, dressed as the Surreal Phantom, and the newspapers of the following day were full of it: the *Evening News* titled it a 'Terrifying Display'; the *Daily Mail* wrote about 'Girl Subjects of Surrealist Paintings', while the *Daily Mirror* featured on page two a 'story' written by their 'Special Correspondent':

The absence of a pork chop almost spoiled the dress of a 'phantom mannequin' who – in spite of the chop's absence, was the sensation of the *International Exhibition of Surrealists* (artists who do the queerest of pictures) at the New Burlington Galleries, London. A pork chop was all she needed to perfect her Surrealist dress of rosebuds, coral shoes, masked hands, face and ears and surgical rubber gloves fitting to the elbows. So, at the last minute she was given a dummy leg from a dressmaker's shop, covered with a silk stocking. With this she paraded up and down during the opening ceremony. The phantom mannequin is Miss Sheila Legge, well-known artist in Surrealist circles in London and Paris. Everyone was deadly serious about Miss Legge and her pork-chop substitute. Those who understood what she was 'phantoming' cocked their heads and nodded in disapproval. Those who went to find out what Surrealism is, came away shocked, amused, scared or just bored.[1]

To the average Londoner, this kind of notoriety was what constituted Surrealism: the reporting of the bizarre approaches to dress of many of the artists.

Even from its very beginnings, formulated by André Breton in 1924, the accoutrements of dress were central to the expressive potential of Surrealism. Breton's poem of 1919, *La Corset mystère*, was formed from overheard remarks by Parisian shoppers as they passed under a painted sign advertising a corset; many of Max Ernst's collages were taken from illustrated fashion magazines, while many of Man Ray's photographs used props familiar to a fashion photographer's studio (and he also published many a fashion photograph). But it was not until the mid-1930s that Surrealism began to influence the sphere of fashion – the designs of the Italian-born fashion designer Elsa Schiaparelli and her famous collaborations made with members of the Surrealist group such as Man Ray, Dalí and Oppenheim being the most obvious. Schiaparelli's career bears out the delayed reaction from fashion to the possibilities of Surrealism; she did not begin her career in Paris until 1928 (four years after the first *Manifesto of Surrealism*), and did not excel into her creative prime until the mid-1930s, with her London shop on Upper Grosvenor Street opening in November 1933.

The gap of twelve years between André Breton's *Manifesto of Surrealism* developed in Paris (1924) and the arrival of the *International*

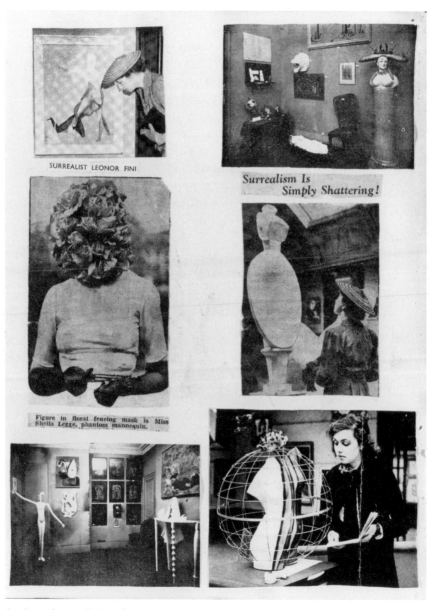

Within the collage:

SURREALIST LEONOR FINI

Surrealism Is Simply Shattering!

Figure in floral fencing mask is Miss Sheila Legge, phantom mannequin.

A collage of press clippings featuring the *International Surrealist Exhibition* at the New Burlington Galleries, London, 1936.

Surrealist Exhibition in London (1936) is thought to underline how British artists lagged behind their European counterparts in the reformulation of artistic trends. Even though the exhibition was part of a wider programme of events organized by Breton and Paul Eluard to widen the international status of Surrealism as an art movement, the criticisms levied at the flourishing of Surrealism in Britain were mainly for how it quickly became subsumed into a decorative language that was applied as a fashionable veneer to amuse and titillate rather than to upset and disturb: a collusion where the provocation of the surreal object was converted into the visual persuasion of a commodity for sale. Surprisingly, one finds evidence of these divisions articulated in the issue of the *International Surrealist Bulletin* published to coincide with the exhibition:

> For some years past a number of individuals have taken a certain interest in the work of the Surrealist movement abroad; but it is necessary to point out that in many cases this interest has been the idle curiosity of the dilettanti, and that these people now proclaim, gratuitously, that Surrealism is a 'fashion', that it is merely 'amusing' or 'out of date'; some of them realise, perhaps, that an effective Surrealist movement would menace the pretensions of litterateurs and aesthetes, and they therefore try to discredit our activity by limiting Surrealism to a certain time and place: by relegating it to the Paris of the 1920s.[2]

The statement suggests that the dissemination of British Surrealism through the channels of fashion would limit its potential as a 'serious' movement; but to side with the statement denies the interesting timing of the 1936 exhibition as crystallizing the relationship between Surrealism as an artistic practice and its influence on fashionable dress.

The parallel developments between Surrealist art and Surrealist dress at this time are bound by gendered distinctions. As the British press reports demonstrate, what was first noticeable to the untrained eye were not the artworks, but the many female artists associated with them. The male artists, although surreal, were much more sober in the way they traded upon sartorial codes of male dress. Put simply, Dalí's jacket or his deep-sea diving outfit do not disturb us as much as Legge's Phantom. When Dalí was rescued from near suffocation his clothes were so soaked in sweat that his wife Gala ran to Savile Row to buy him something to wear as a change of dress. This is not without significance.

The proximity of Savile Row to Cork Street, which runs parallel, and to Burlington Gardens, which joins them both, is of some importance in explaining this gendered distinction in the expression of Surrealism in London. It articulates the fixed and static qualities of male artistic dress within the Surrealists as associated with the long-standing fitting-rooms of Savile Row, and the mobile and animated qualities of female artistic dress as associated with the galleries of Cork Street and Burlington Gardens, with their colourful changing programmes of temporary exhibitions. What they profitably demonstrate is that in the gendered approaches towards the promotion of Surrealism in Britain, each was equivalent in scale to the layout of the Mayfair streets.

It is recognized that the central concern of women Surrealists was the presentation of women as objects of male need and how this diverged from their desire to assert their individuality and self-expression. One of the most celebrated objects at the 1936 exhibition was Meret Oppenheim's *Le Déjeuner en fourrure*. Beyond its ultimate power as an object of fascination and repulsion, the disguised function of a teacup, saucer and spoon covered in fur was quickly absorbed into a male-oriented discourse of Surrealism, because it was chiefly an object associated with the domestic sphere. What is unusual about many of the examples I am going to consider is that they are constructed from the social, metropolitan sphere of women, rather than the domestic one.

In the now famous photograph of the Group of Surrealists taken just before the opening of the exhibition, the women sit while the men stand, their differences articulated by gender and dress. Sheila Legge wears a loosely structured black silk jacket with a corsage at the neck, black gloves and matching strap-heeled sandals, while Eileen Agar, the other notable woman exhibiting, wears a knitted Tyrolean-style hat designed by Schiaparelli with a tubular pointed top and a light-coloured,

A group of Surrealists at the New Burlington Galleries, London, 1936, during the *International Surrealist Exhibition*.

form-fitting tailored jacket with extended collars and raised sleeve-heads. Agar was later to summarize her pronounced interest in dress as a mode of communication for her artistic beliefs as a woman:

> The Surrealist women, whether painters or not, were equally good-looking. They were elegant and dressed with panache, caring about clothes and their surroundings, however strange the interiors. Our concern with appearance was not as a result of pandering to masculine demands, but rather a shared attitude to life and style.
>
> This was in striking contrast to the other professional woman painters of the time, those who were not Surrealists, who if seen

at all, tended to flaunt their art like a badge, appearing in deliberately paint-spotted clothing. The juxtaposition by us of a Schiaparelli dress with outrageous behaviour or conversation was simply carrying the beliefs of Surrealism into public existence.[3]

The purpose of Agar's appearance was to act as a badge of membership of Surrealism, while actively contesting the conventions of the everyday. While the results of the collaborations that Schiaparelli fostered with male artists such as Dalí and Jean Cocteau are considered to be heightened and covetable aspects of dress design informed by artistic practice, the relation that artists bear to such objects when wearing them is rarely considered.

The hat that Agar wears in the 1936 photograph assumes a particular significance in that it also appears in two important documents that relate to Schiaparelli's acceptance by the Surrealists in Paris and her infamy in the British fashion press. The first, Tristan Tzara's essay 'Of a Certain Automatism of Taste', which was published in the Surrealist magazine *Minotaure* in Paris in 1933, discusses the symbolic associations made by three of Schiaparelli's hat designs, which are illustrated with photographs by Man Ray. The second is a fashion illustration by Cecil Beaton in British *Vogue* of April 1935, which shows Schiaparelli's spring fashion show in which a number of the items bear a printed textile design composed of a collage of press cuttings collated from her previous collection.[4]

Of the three hats illustrated in Tzara's essay, the first is a man's and is called 'Savile Row', the second is the kind worn by Agar titled 'The Mad Cap' (looking at the photograph the model could be Agar) and the third is worn by Schiaparelli herself and is called 'The Crazy Coxcomb'. While the man's hat is as reserved and refined as its title, the two hats for women are sculptural forms that carry the forms of Surrealism into public existence. Their titles are as much about instability and hysteria as they are about the playfulness of these ideas in terms of the literary reference of the Mad Hatter (further associated in the French term for millinery). As such, they indicate the gendered difference between the ideas for dress formed from the conventions of English tailoring and

Cecil Beaton, illustration of designs by Elsa Schiaparelli, 'Fun at the Openings', in British *Vogue* (1 April 1935).

the ideas of dress drawn from the incongruous forms associated with an art movement.

The suitability of the Mayfair streets already mentioned for containing these gendered practices is central to their definition in the 1930s. In Schiaparelli's printed textile of her own press reviews we get a sense of how provocation was central to the designer's ideas; in a sense, of how important the newsworthiness of her endeavour was to her. For many of the women associated with British Surrealism, this was something that they realized not solely in the spaces of fashion salons or art galleries, but also in the streets as an everyday practice. Schiaparelli understood this principle implicitly as being particular to fashion design and distinct from art:

Hats photographed by Man Ray, in Tristan Tzara's article 'Of a Certain Automatism of Taste' ('D'un certain Automatisme du Goùt') in *Minotaure* (1933).

A dress cannot just hang like a painting on the wall, or like a book remain intact and live a long and sheltered life. A dress has no life of its own unless it is worn, and as soon as this happens another personality takes over from you and animates it, or tries to, glorifies or destroys it, or makes it into a song of beauty.[5]

This gendered distinction did not go unnoticed in the British press. As the *Daily Star* reported at a later Surrealist exhibition on Cork Street in 1937:

Never has there been such a gathering of surrealists. It was a little disappointing to find their appearance was not nearly so exotic as their art. The young men who produced the extraordinary objects exhibited seemed to prefer tweeds and pull-overs to the combination of garments that surrealism seems to call for.[6]

In realizing the notoriety of the female artist through the guise of a fashionable and surreal appearance, the period is important for crystallizing the concerns of the two magazine articles previously mentioned. The suitability of a hat for harnessing these ideas in artistic practice became central to Agar's own work, as we shall see later. Agar confirmed this in her own recollections of the legendary opening:

I remember a sizzling hot day with large crowds streaming upstairs to the third floor where women in light and colourful clothes made a splash in exotic hats either whispering or talking loudly while the men in sober suits or tattered trousers were arguing, gesticulating, disagreeing, looking puzzled or annoyed or enquiring, making introductions that developed into friendship or the reverse.[7]

The galvanizing of fashion and Surrealism by women artists has not been the subject of much scrutiny and yet it remains crucial to an understanding of this art movement in Britain at this juncture. In a page of press cuttings in Eileen Agar's archive the accompanying photographs of the exhibition opening show the Surrealist Phantom's head, some sculptures in the exhibition being looked at by a woman wearing a fashionable hat, and one of Agar's sculptures. As a collage it synthesizes the convergence between artistic practice and the concerns of fashion for female Surrealists in the period. A head of rose blooms becomes a sculpture – becomes a woman's head wearing a hat – becomes a mannequin head. Although the photographic collage should suggest these different forms as incongruous juxtapositions, the way in which they seem to dissolve into each other easily is expressive of their close affinities at this time.

Tristan Tzara's article on the surreal qualities of hat design and hat-wearing in the summer of 1933 identified that much of it was to do with sexual representation; but that what was important was how it was displaced: 'It seems that this world is characterised by valuing the different parts of the body for which embellishment serves both as awning and lure.'[8] Tzara recognized that the language of Surrealism and fashion photography was not that distinct in how it isolated aspects of the female form. He also acknowledged fashionable millinery as a means of extending the form of the female head in a manner that was not too dissimilar from the sculptural experiments of Surrealist artists. (Unbeknown to Tzara, the British Surrealist John Banting was dabbling as an artist and a milliner at the same time.) Put crudely, the article is a fascination with how hats, when photographed in a certain way, look like genitalia. But this was not the first time that hats were exploited by the Surrealists for their expressive forms.

In his study of the centrality of fashion to the literary concept of modernity, Ulrich Lehmann observes that the top hat was one of a limited repertoire of items of apparel that became a consistent metaphor in the mythologizing of the modern by the Surrealists in Paris in the 1920s. The top hat was favoured as a nineteenth-century sartorial expression symbolic of propriety, modesty and industriousness (for the way it could almost resemble a smokestack), but above all mystery. For them it retained its wonder as a ghostly apparition from the past, a haunting aesthetic symbol for the present.

In contrast, the kind of hat that represents London in the 1930s is materially understood as surreal, as if a label has been stitched into the interior seam of the hat bearing the word Surrealism as the maker's mark. Rather than having a form that is consistent, it is amorphous. Instead of being for men, it is for women; instead of being serious, it is playful. Instead of the nineteenth century transposed, it is constructed with the intention of the moment; instead of being illustrated, it is photographed. It has a literalness about its Surrealism that the top hat is able to resist. It very much supports the curator Richard Martin's belief that 'fashion and its instruments were at the heart of the Surrealist metaphor, touching on the imagery of woman and the correlation between the world of real objects and the life of objects in the mind'.[9] And yet the fashionably surreal hat of 1930s is more fully realized when related to the broader culture of the period, very much concerned with presentation of the female face and the framing of it by various means.

It was a culture informed by the close-up, a film shot developed in popular American cinema to concentrate on the facial contours of the hero or heroine to aid identification by the viewer and to support the Hollywood star system. And the proportions in which these faces appeared, projected onto the screen in cinemas, propagated an attention to detail in the face's exquisite potential for self-expression, often by modified means. The flawless complexion, arched brows and smouldering lips originally painted onto an actress's face so that her expressions would register when captured on celluloid film had now been refined into a formal cosmetic language that was eagerly copied by women. Through the principle of the close-up and the industrial manufacture and marketing of cosmetics, what had once been socially unacceptable was transformed into a means of everyday self-presentation. What had once been a sign of a debased social other, namely the painted woman, had become an affordable element in the purchasing of feminine identity as style. (The tattooist George Burchett had by now turned his studio into a beauty parlour and was making a living offering permanent tattooed make-up for women.)

Salvador Dalí's painting *The Face of Mae West (Usable as a Surrealist Apartment)* (1934–5) paid its dues to the scale of the cinematic close-up by scaling the actress's face as large as a formal room, transforming her lips into a sofa, which was made a Surrealist motif for the application and displacement of desire. (The sofa had originally been an actual commission from the British art patron Edward James for his home in Wimpole Street.) If a women wearing lipstick was to be understood anthropologically as bearing a sign of sexual poise, then the idea of reclining on an oversized object of a similar shape was a provocative invitation. While James had his sofas covered in felt, those commissioned by Schiaparelli for her showrooms were produced in 'Shocking Pink' satin, Dalí's original specification, which in turn became the shade of puce lipstick for which the couturier became renowned. (Although James was known as being one of Schiaparelli's best customers at her London salon, his reputation for being a very later payer is thought to be one of the reasons why she closed her London store in 1939.)

The centring of self-expression on the face was also to be demonstrated by the dominance of portraiture as the principle genre of the period, whether in painting or the plastic arts, new forms of biography or the reported interest in new forms of celebrity. Much of this was informed by photographic representation. Cecil Beaton's roaming style of portraiture (he possessed no studio) did much to popularize the modern female subject from a London viewpoint. His photographs of society ladies transformed – through cast shadows, greased cheeks, reflections from silver paper and implausible props – into uncharacteristic, modern subjects replicated another form of close-up. Such importance was placed on this form of representation that the glossy society weekly *The Sphere*, which published many of these photographs, named the subjects 'the photocracy': a new form of status driven purely by the modern manner of representation centred on the face.

Eileen Agar was herself no stranger to this kind of depiction; in 1927 she had posed for Beaton against a backdrop tiled with foil panels and the broad expressive brushstrokes of the theatrical set designer. Beaton casts her as a notable beauty for her prominent bone structure and broad eyes, which were so desirable for the time, although without any visual reference to her own artistic credentials. Notably, this photograph sits in stark contrast to any other photograph of Agar, where her artistic identity is always rendered and maintained.

Another link unknown to them at the time was that both Beaton and Agar were enthralled as children by Lily Elsie, the actress who wore costumes designed by Lucile in *The Merry Widow* (1907). For Beaton, it was her image on a postcard that began his love of glamour when he saw it first as a child; for Agar it was in her mother's decision (who also wore Lucile) not to allow her daughters to be bridesmaids at Elsie's wedding. They demonstrate how this theatrical definition of embellished femininity from the early part of the twentieth century bore heavily on Beaton's and Agar's depictions of modern experience; and it is here that the hat once again plays a central role.

Agar's mother was a keen follower of fashion, as befitted a woman bringing up a family in Mayfair and who played bridge with Margot Asquith. Her collection of hats was the subject of endless fascination for

Eileen Agar
photographed by
Cecil Beaton, 1927.

her daughter, with more than forty hats once taken to a stay at the seaside: 'And what hats! Enormous constructions of straw, velvet or fur like frigates under sail or birds on the wing, embellished with vast bows, ribbons or ostrich feathers.'[10] For Beaton, the overblown proportions of *The Merry Widow* hat never faded in his mind, and eventually became the crowning glory of his costume design for the film *My Fair Lady*, which won him an Oscar. In many of Beaton's portraits published in fashion magazines in the 1930s, the hat becomes the means by which he elevates his subject through the status of fashion, or lampoons through the association with theatricality. Much of this published work crafts modern femininity by its very otherness – an old-fashioned otherness moulded from the techniques of theatrical fancy. As a strategy it was also employed by Agar. The hat then, in its use by both practitioners, becomes the motif of Surrealism and the theatrical imagination condensed.

The publication of John Banting's book of illustrated poems, *A Blue Book of Conversation* (1946), cemented further the potential for the surreal hat, with other attributes of dress, successfully to lampoon the immoral vacancy of British society. For a short time himself a milliner and a window-dresser for a number of London stores, Banting based his publication on drawings and observations he had been recording since the 1930s of society life and the fashion world. Although he is construed as a somewhat marginal figure of British Surrealism, Banting's own contribution to the everyday practice of Surrealism through self-expression informed by dress is unusual for a male artist. As Agar recalled: 'from time to time he dyed his hair green, or cut off the tops of his shoes to show his painted toe-nails – in homage to Magritte of course'. It was reported by the *Daily Mail* that Banting was rejected from the *International Surrealist Exhibition* on account of taking the liberation of Surrealism too far. He was, however, one of the few British artists to practise what could be considered Surrealist art some time before 1936 on account of the visits to Paris he had made with Nancy Cunard. Some British artists, though, found that they had no need to go to Europe to learn of new ideas, so near were these ideas to their doorsteps.

Hampstead had had an artistic colony since the time of Constable, but in the 1930s it benefited from the influx of eminent European émigrés who cultivated an intellectual life that attracted many. Crucial modernist artists such as Piet Mondrian and Naum Gabo rented homes there; architects including Erno Goldfinger and Berthold Lubetkin built homes for themselves and others in the area; while the Isokon Building on Lawn Road designed by Wells Coates harboured the cream of the Bauhaus, including Marcel Breuer, Walter Gropius and László Moholy-Nagy. The network of intellectual residences in Hampstead in the 1930s turned a leafy retreat not far from central London into a refuge for the European avant-garde; it served as a microcosm of the Continent for the fertile exchange of intellectual ideas, wholly foreign for London.

Roland Penrose's house on Downshire Hill became the meeting place for a small coterie of artists, poets and writers who either lived or socialized in Hampstead. Sheila Legge's lover was David Gascoyne, a young poet and critic who was the first to raise the possibility of a British response to Surrealism, publishing *A Short Survey of Surrealism* in 1935. With Roland Penrose and Lee Miller, they began to meet with Humphrey Jennings, Herbert Read, Paul Nash, Eileen Agar, E.L.T. Mesens and others, indulging in 'séances of automatic writing and *cadavre exquis* drawings'.[11] It must have been at one of these convivial meetings that Gascoyne came-up with the idea of transposing a figure from Salvador Dalí's recent painting *Three Young Surrealist Women Holding in Their Arms the Skins of an Orchestra* (1936) into a costume for Legge to adopt as a ghostly persona for the forthcoming London exhibition they were planning.

Dalí's painting depicts three women who have heads of flower blooms and wear pale coloured dresses, one of which bears tear marks as if made from paper. (The *trompe-l'œil* quality of the painted dress design was later reconfigured by Dalí into a printed textile design for Elsa Schiaparelli, famously used in her 'Tear Dress' of 1938, while the figures in the paintings were also to be reworked by Dalí for a cover of American *Vogue* in June 1939.) On a simple level, Legge's costume is the presentation of a painting come to life. As a piece of performance it is a female Surrealist artist posing in the tradition of *tableaux vivant*, and as such it is novel for the old-fashioned sense of theatricality it poses to what would have been considered a very modern painting. Yet in being presented in terms of a fashionable outfit for a woman to wear, the piece has other implications.

With its fashionable silhouette, fine fabric and sugary colour, Legge's dress appears to have divested itself of the flora it should be bearing, which has instead floated upwards to form the contours of what should be her head. Unlike the faces of the sixteenth-century artist Arcimboldo, painted as if the features are elaborately constructed from a cornucopia of fruit and vegetables, the uniformity of the rose blooms and their placement suggest an egg-like sphere flowering rather than a human head. It equates the occasions for wearing formal dress for women with the highpoint of a bloom in a plant's cycle. Yet the underlying sugges-

Vogue cover by Salvador Dalí,
1 June 1939.

Salvador Dalí, *Three Young Surrealist
Women Holding in Their Arms the Skins
of an Orchestra*, 1936, oil on canvas.

tion is that the floral blooms that should adorn the dress as decoration have now solely become the woman's social expression. She becomes an immutable object of desire, a rise to *l'amour fou* as the Surrealists liked to call it, but she remains encumbered and encased by the expressiveness of her allure.

The outfit is a playful wavering between the flora and fauna deployed by fashion and its use as a Surrealist trope. In turning a painted depiction of a surreal woman into a living one, Legge may have seemingly pointed to the absurdity of the proposition, but she also underlined the social inadequacy of the role proposed for the surreal woman. In veiling her head with rose blooms, Legge denies her own identity but maintains her own celebrity; she maintains her role as muse, but denies her own subjectivity. Her costume can therefore be understood as a proposition to the role of women in Surrealism: as a floriate but mute kind of femininity.

While the Surrealist Phantom's outfit was just as provocative as Dalí's deep-sea diving suit, they both indicate a gendered difference in the use of costume to connote the surreal. Dalí's use was to play up absurdly the incongruous and inappropriate use of a functional garment, while Legge's outfit trades upon the tropes of fashionable dress to raise the possibility of disturbance. Removed from the context of the sea, Dalí's outfit is so heavy he is unable to move in it, whereas the floriate figure of the Surreal Phantom haunts not only the corridors of the New Burlington Galleries, but also the streets of London.

The haunting and unsettling photograph of Legge wearing the outfit in Trafalgar Square, attributed to the Surrealist photographer Claude Cahun, remains the most defiant image of the fashionable and surreal woman as phantom, walking unaided, as if blinded by the notion of beauty. The power of the image remains undiminished: the surreal woman disengaged from a surreal environment already has an alienating quality, but it is even more startling when set against a recognized landmark. It maintains itself as one of the earliest examples of surreal displacement so favoured by fashion photographers to evoke the unworldly qualities of fashion against the seeming incongruity of the everyday.

Sheila Legge as 'phantom mannequin' in Trafalgar Square, 1936.

Cahun herself has been re-established only recently into the Surrealist canon for the photographs she took of herself from 1919, the year that she consciously abandoned the visual conventions of femininity by shaving her head and sometimes dying it in bright colours. Much of her personal work is concerned with the otherness of femininity and the notion of performing herself through fractured, multiplicitous identities. Taking this into account, the close-up photograph of Legge in

Trafalgar Square, which was not used in the publicity for the *International Surrealist Exhibition* (a wider shot including more of the square was used on the cover of the fourth issue of the *International Surrealist Bulletin*), bears the preoccupations of more than one female Surrealist.

The surreal expression of a woman blinded by beauty is also to be found in the homes of Edward James, who had his house on Wimpole Street decorated to please his wife, the actress Lily Tosch (who was also keenly photographed and painted by Beaton). Not content with giving her a bathroom designed by Paul Nash, he had his decorator take this principle further by designing a carpet for his country home, West

Detail of Tilly Losch footprint carpet, West Dean, Sussex, installed in the 1930s.

Dean, that bore a motif based on her footprints, appearing as if she had traipsed wet from the bathroom throughout the house.

Surrealism in Britain had its next outing at the London Gallery on Cork Street, which had been taken over by Roland Penrose and the bookseller Anton Zwemmer in April 1936. The exhibition *Surrealist Objects and Poems* in 1937 was as press-worthy as the last and included two works by Agar, one featuring on the catalogue cover. The first head, *Angel of Anarchy* (now lost), was a plaster bust covered in black fur, green feathers and white doileys to demarcate the different contours of the face. The second, *Rococo Cocotte* (destroyed), was a classical plaster bust with a plume of black ostrich feathers for hair, a black felt moustache and paste buckles on black ribbon for eyes, looking as if swathed in wrap-around glasses. Here Agar applied the lexicon of feminine materials drawn from theatrical costume, in the style of the savage, to a sculpture produced according to the masculine conventions of art practice. It produced a brutal kind of beauty. It is accepted by many that the blindfolded head was intended to convey the uncertainty of mankind; yet the uncertainty is as much about the gender ambiguity raised by the materials that are applied to its surface.

This appears most potently in the second version of *Angel of Anarchy*. Here, the front of the head is blindfolded in a broad band of blue silk; at the back it sprouts a head of ostrich feathers bearing African beads, a swath of dark cloth around the neck and a nose studded with diamante. The power of the object is that although it looks bound and mute, it is defiant: blind to civilized beauty, but beautiful by all that is uncivilized. It is the threat and allure of female desire as surreal, transposed to an obscure object. According to the *Daily Sketch*, the exhibition was opened at midnight

> by an 'explorer' wearing a sun-helmet, red gloves and enormous dark glasses with mirror-glass lenses. On his chest was a placard inscribed 'Totally Blind'. Surrealist Eileen Agar wore cream gloves with scarlet cloth tips like fingernails. Another girl had a blond neck-bun attached to her own dark hair.[12]

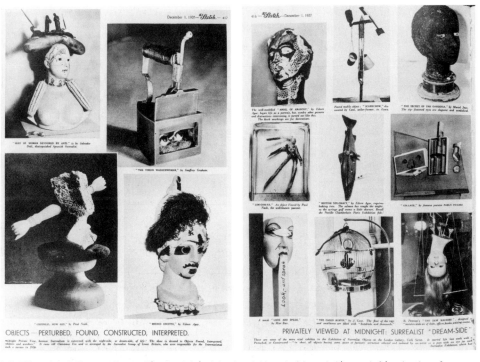

left: Eileen Agar's 'Rococo Cocotte' (lower right); *right*: Agar's 'Angel of Anarchy' (upper left), selections from an *Exhibition of Surrealist Objects* at the London Gallery, Cork Street, in *The Sketch*, 1 December 1937.

Sheila Legge attended wearing a black satin skirt pinned up with a large safety pin, to display tattooed calves and an eye winking wickedly from the back of one knee (in deference to that old-fashioned vogue for tattooing). The gloves that Agar wore were designed by Schiaparelli, which the artist teamed with a Mario Fortuny pleated silk dress in bright blue – a combination that would have been more than striking. The gloves themselves were, in turn, to become the source material for her sculpture *Glove Hat* (c.1936).

In visually quoting surreal items of apparel within her own art-works, Agar conflated the ephemeral with the immutable, born from her own experience of wearing the gloves and her wish to memorialize them. In bearing the traces of being worn, in the limp, distended quality of the leather, the gloves are reminiscent of the tubular skin that a snake sheds, an abject hollow – perhaps a remnant of a once social skin. The brutal manner in which they are pinned to the rush hat, as if nailed in the style of a crucifixion by the jewelled head of a hatpin, underlines their presentation as lifeless things that once constituted her self-expression. Thus, in presenting her own social skin as a piece of ornament applied to the crown of a hat that poses as an art object, Agar tells us that the documentation of her life as a surreal artist is, literally, what underpins her creative practice.

Agar's hats propose that the wearing of fashionable Surrealism was a way of displacing the male gaze by embracing the themes of otherness, theatricality, parody and wit as a form of resistance and deflection. Further, her decorated heads resist the male gaze by the talismans they are adorned with: so they are pierced by appliqué, bound by threaded beads, blinded by diamante, tarred with fur and feathers.

Glove Hat, Eileen Agar, c. 1936.

British Surrealism was indeed measured in Britain by the reaction of the national press. The fourth issue of the *International Surrealist Bulletin*, published after the occasion of the 1936 exhibition, took the opportunity to give scathing, detailed analyses of press reportage across a range of newspaper titles. Although it proves that from the very outset British Surrealism measured its superiority by its dismissal of the national press, it understood that it could communicate its ideas only by entertaining it. Much of the inventiveness on the part of the national press in its reaction to British Surrealism has been forgotten with the passage of time, which is a shame since much of it trades upon an indigenous humour and eccentricity that have become the lasting features of what constitutes a national expression of this art movement.

One of the most famous fashion photographs to draw upon Surrealism is Man Ray's photograph of his padded wheelbarrow containing a model reclining in a Lucien Lelong dress, which was published in *Harper's Bazaar* in 1937. The sculpture also featured in the London Gallery's exhibition of the same year, where it became the central subject in an article by the *Daily Star*:

> There seemed only one thing lacking from the Surrealist Exhibition at the London Gallery to-day. The public, admitted free, were not surrealist enough. Conventional fur coats, maudlin linen collars, fantastic trousers and what not. So I took my friend Smithy in with me. He is a dustman and he and his mates were functioning with their usual élan in Cork Street. Smithy demurred at first, but when I told him anybody could go he said he was on. And a lovely surrealist note he made too, with his almost invisible face, his vast blue smock, huge leggings, coalman's hat and leather gauntlet gloves, the whole surmounted by the battered dustbin he has banged down on the pavement a thousand times.[13]

Smithy ends up so enjoying himself that he wants to buy the wheelbarrow sculpture for his daughter because 'she wanted something modern for her drawing room'. The idea of a dustman wheeling out the barrow to take home to his daughter is very funny, but the report does underline the centrality of dress to the expression of Surrealism in London. With his almost invisible face (not unlike Sheila Legge's when she appeared as the Surreal Phantom), Smithy is cast as a character that performs Surrealism rather than just a spectator who merely observes it. He is surreal for looking extraordinary when doing the most ordinary of his daily tasks. And this is what women Surrealists were also particularly good at. This was taken to its logical conclusion by a short BBC feature of 1948 featuring Agar showing her 1936 artwork *Hat for Eating Bouillabaisse*: the important point being that it was not filmed in a gallery, but with Agar wearing it while going about her weekly shop.

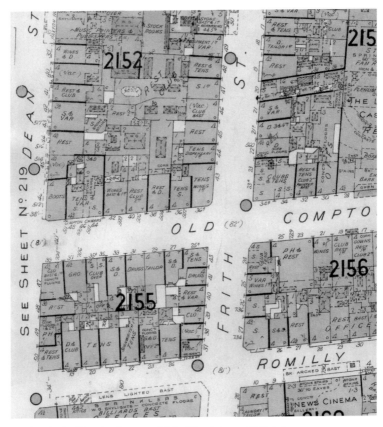

Fire Regulation Map showing part of Soho (Sheet FIP IX.226), October 1944.

CHAPTER FOUR

In the 1948 film of Eileen Agar wearing her Hat for Eating
Bouillabaisse, there is another, post-war layer of the absurd:
bouillabaisse was largely impossible to make, or even eat, in
food-rationed London. World War Two brought irrevocable
change to London life in the smallest of details. Contrary to the
abundance of Agar's hat was austerity. This chapter deals with
the impact of war on artistic dress for men in London and
concentrates primarily on the artist Francis Bacon. The memory
of male Surrealist artists in their paint-spattered jackets in 1936
must now have seemed very odd, given that the dishevelled look
was then a conscious choice. Every London man was now familiar
with the degradation of his wardrobe, constrained by rationing
and held together by make-do-and-mend. The wartime restrictions placed on the sale of textiles and clothing were lifted only in
1951, so dress remained an important visual indicator of scarcity
in the metropolis. What it also bore at this time was the possibility
of demonstrating how one could temporarily resist austerity,
either through the wearing of black market goods that flourished
for sale on most street corners, or though the adoption of a style
that appeared in disregard of the 'common cause'. This style
can be understood as a post-war departure of artistic dress
in extremis. And it is concerned with an artist who bore the
weight of his existence not only in his work but also in his dress –
carrying his painterly wounds upon his raggedy back.

London, ravaged, if not razed by the Blitz, carved new pathways through the city; it bared an unrecognizable skyline, revealed long-lost vistas and exposed things long since sedimented. Post-war reconstruction was far from immediate and London life was conducted betwixt and between this new-found archaeology of the city. The deregulation this temporarily brought offered libertines a new understanding of the broken city as a bountiful prospect. Even long after the bomb damage had been eradicated, the memory that bound deprivation and illicit opportunity together was an important catalyst for the definition of post-war experience.

Many of the intellectual émigrés who had contributed to British Surrealism across the span of the 1930s had now moved to America to engage in its aesthetic of plenty and its prospect of opportunity. Those who remained as British subjects were drafted in to help with the war effort: Roland Penrose helped design British camouflage for the Army, but still managed to paint the body of his wife, Lee Miller, to test how well it concealed the human form. The role that Francis Bacon played in picking up the threads of enquiry established by British Surrealism is well captured by the art historian Helen Lessore's famous declaration that Bacon emerged as an artist as if

> coming into the theatre in the middle of a play without knowing the language, but so immediately and intuitively sensing what the drama is about that, quickly picking up a few words and phrases in the current idiom – which happened to be Surrealism – he at once, as if sleepwalking, steps on to the stage and begins to take part – even an important part – in the performance.[1]

The sense of theatrical performance that Lessore implies is very important to an understanding of Bacon as a character of London life in the immediate post-war period.

Whereas new debates about the nature of post-war culture were informed by the American aesthetic of plenty, albeit in distanced terms; Bacon advocated his own aesthetic of plenty, except that it was located in a small district of central London known as Soho. His notion of plenty

John Deakin, *Portrait of Francis Bacon*, c. 1952, photograph.

was captured in his embrace of the visual and carnal delights of London, which serviced his daily performance of what it was to be an artist.

The French existential sculptor Alberto Giacometti once told Bacon in the back of a London taxi: 'When I'm in London, I feel homosexual.'[2] He was praising his fellow artist on a fully cultivated lifestyle that bonded a social coterie to an area of central London by the excessive consumption of fine drink, good food and keen observation. This feeling that Giacometti identified was for him perceptibly grafted to the experience of *being* in London, in particular being with Bacon and his cohorts in and around the area of Soho.

The statement may well have been informed by many things: Soho's historical sedimentation of interest by homosexual men, the emerging drag of men's dress to the west of Soho, the camp posturing of the coffee-bar scene, the prevailing atmosphere of tolerance and mischief in the capital's post-war playground. Yet to take this opinion is perhaps to expect too much of an artist who had led a sheltered existence and was only briefly introduced to London and Bacon by Isabel Rawsthorne, a model and friend of both artists. In a sense, we can appreciate how Giacometti was essentially complimenting the artist on a sense of *being* largely understood through appearance.

Bacon believed and made it well known of his view that homosexuals possessed a discriminating eye for how people carried themselves, a heightened awareness not so much expressed by a lingering gaze but by a swift approximation – to bring things down to their essential element in sum, or to be reduced further to a mere detail. He claimed homosexuals as being

> obsessed with the physique. They simply never stop looking at the body, all of it, the whole time, and pulling it to pieces. That's why if I ever wanted to know what someone really looks like, I've always asked a queer. They're ruthless and precise.[3]

This special skill demanded its own forms of verbal support, communicated by the coded language of Polari, where *vada* (to look) seems to predicate every utterance.

As a way of seeing, distinct parallels can be drawn with Bacon's own resolutions for the painted depiction of the male figure, but this is to miss the centrality of the artist's own appearance, of which he was obsessed, and its inter-dependent animation by the streets of Soho. Art historians such as Amelia Jones have more recently considered artistic male dress as performative, a staged presentation of masculinity that is nurtured rather than natural. Much of this work centres upon the photographic documentation of artists at work in their studios, but has expanded to those artists who use self-presentational performance as a means of expression.

To complement the numerous books on the subject of Bacon's art, there is now a publishing trend that examines the social history of Soho as a panorama of city life that privileges a range of masculine personalities. Drawn from literary, artistic and youth-related avenues, they fervidly recount the tawdry shops of illicit pleasures, ethnic restaurants and wood-panelled pubs. Figures such as Daniel Farson are central to recounting the post-war experience of Soho as a kind of oral fiction about drunken nights; the photographer John Deakin's portfolio, recently resuscitated by Robin Muir, is in tatters and mainly undated, while Nigel Richardson's *Dog Days in Soho: One Man's Adventures in Fifties Bohemia* takes the scant biographical details of the sailor Josh Avery's life and with a few pieces of photographic evidence springs a story to semi-fictional life.

The blurred and ill-defined edges of these things render the allure of Soho as 'a voluptuous nightmare whose protagonists rushed ever more desperately through those dark alleyways'.[4] For Bacon and his acquaintances, this was to be a language of masculinity conditioned by post-war austerity, but celebrated through artistic licentiousness and at odds with the newly wrought construction of the 'man about town' as put forward by Tailor & Cutter's new trade magazine of that name. Rather, it traded on earlier models of masculinity: it expected the requisite pleasures of the dandy; it was comforted by the plush luxuries of the Edwardian gentleman; it demanded the uninhibited desires of the Weimar days of Berlin; it affected the limitless credit of the aristocracy; it was informed and repeatedly indulged by the *flâneur's* sport of visual spectatorship.

The strictly enforced routine of Bacon's London life, well documented, suggests that his daily movements can be thought of as a series of linked situations that plot the artist's path across the city. By doing this they can be compared to the great tradition of a life expressed in printed pictures. They demand a scrutiny not unlike that given to Hogarth's depiction of the downfall of a man of easy virtue in *The Rake's Progress* (1735), the prescribed advice that D. T. Egerton dispensed to the London Dandy of the 1820s, and the satirical lampooning of the post-war cultured male in Ronald Searle's *Rake's Progress*, serialized in *Punch* magazine in the 1950s.

The mythology of Bacon in London begins not in the 'gilded squalor' of post-war Soho, but rather earlier in South Kensington. His output as a designer and decorator was the first to bring him a degree of notoriety, displayed in a studio comprising a converted garage with living quarters above that he rented on Queensbury Mews West. It was his first performance in setting out a space as a set for modern living, swiftly named 'The 1930 Look in British Decoration' by *Studio Magazine*:

> Francis Bacon is a young English decorator who has worked in Paris and in Germany for some years and is now established in London. We have perhaps been slower than other nations in adapting ourselves to new ideas in furnishings and decoration, but are gradually becoming accustomed to discriminating between what is really good and new in modernist interiors and what is new and bad.[5]

Bacon's discriminating eye had obviously fallen on the experiments of Charlotte Perriand in tubular steel and the amply proportioned forms of Eileen Gray's furniture in Paris. What was really good and new about it for the *Studio* was not necessarily the furniture, but that it was housed in a newly converted studio. The areas of Kensington and Chelsea were still speckled with the efforts of aesthetic artists who had proved themselves adept at forwarding interior decoration tastes from the confines of their studios. Although dimensionally similar, Bacon's studio was appreciated for its modernist articulation. The aesthetic layering of dado, panel and paper was eschewed in favour of bare white

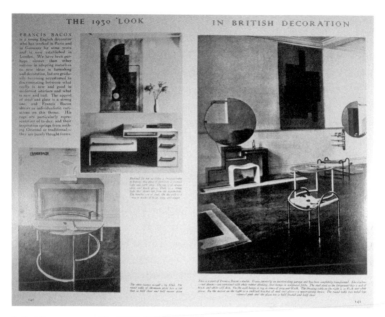

A double-page spread from *The Studio*, August 1930.

walls, save a vertically hung rug, and windows curtained with white rubber sheeting that hung in sculptural folds. As such, the studio was an open-plan space more akin to the architecturally prescribed 'machines for living' than the majority of London studios.

Its fashionability as a space made it an important calling card for commissions, garnered from introductions made at parties that Bacon threw regularly, where 'the cocktail bracket of steel and glass' that he had designed as 'a space saving device' became as well known as his dry martinis. It was after one of these parties that Madge Garland, Editor of British *Vogue*, made the decision to install white rubber curtains in her Mount Street apartment. As we know, Bacon quickly abandoned decoration in favour of painting: *Crucifixion*, painted in 1933, attracted the attention of Herbert Read, and its reproduction in his book *Art Now: An Introduction to the Theory of Modern Painting and Sculpture* (1936) began his artistic career. Yet the fashionable, designed interior was to remain constant to his painted vision.

In Bacon's painted view of the human condition, the setting is the spartan stage of the modern interior: tubular steel predominates, be it formed into cages, the structure of seating, the basis for a perch or a rail beside a bed. The rubber curtains express themselves in vertical lines that enclose and isolate the *mise-en-scène*, while polished surfaces and circular mirrors reflect an inescapable existence. Without a trace of irony, the art critic Adrian Searle touched on the centrality of this setting in reviewing David Sylvester's exhibition of 1998 titled *Francis Bacon: The Human Body*: 'They could have called it *Bacon and Interior Design: From Soft Furnishings To Wall Coverings*, and it wouldn't have made a jot of difference.'[6]

However, the figure does play a central role in Bacon's works, but more often than not through a process of distortion. John Berger was the first to note that while 'the body is usually distorted, whereas what clothes or surrounds it is relatively undistorted. Compare the raincoat with the torso, the umbrella with the arm, the cigarette stub with the mouth.[7] So, it is the illustrated details of modern life that anchor the human condition to the post-war experience in Bacon's paintings: the materials of the domestic interior formed from his own studio and the materials of the dressed exterior noticed by his own eye. While the body fragments and dissolves, all we are left with are the details of visual discourses that pertain to masculinity and the interior.

Much of Bacon's painted works depict a kind of contamination between character and decor. In the case of Bacon's own studio as a working environment, the contamination was here at its most evident. Painters of the late nineteenth century had been quick to adopt the photograph of the artist in his studio as a calling card for gaining commissions and for raising their perceived status. Later studies of this, such as Alexander Liberman's *The Artist in His Studio* (1960), very much set the studio as an environment that enabled and enriched the creative process (for example, a photograph of bottles of turpentine on Giacometti's studio table would echo the undulating forms of his sculptural maquettes of similar size). Bacon was to take this further by making his studio a materialization of his working process to such an extent that it did not require his presence.

Francis Bacon, *Figure Study II*, 1945–6, oil on canvas.

In a photograph by John Deakin of Bacon's lover George Dyer, Dyer stands in the middle of the studio in nothing but his under-pants, surrounded by the detritus of creativity. The mirror designed in 1930 is now aged, its silvering pock-marked, its contours feathered with brushstrokes of paint; it reflects a cramped space flung with books, sodden rags, magazines and paint-laden brushes set into tin cans. Dyer was frequently memorialized in paintings in this vulnerable state, but his lack of clothing points to Bacon's own use of the accoutrements of

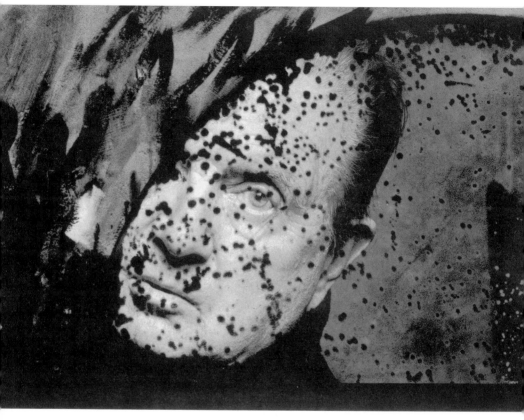

Francis Giacobetti, *Francis Bacon (Portrait in the Mirror)*, 1991, photograph.

male dress for his own artistic methods; so that 'paint-soaked socks and cashmere sweaters' were often to be found around the studio, 'the latter much prized for the delicate ribbing effect they produced when pressed on the canvas'.[8] This contamination of dress into image was central to Bacon's attitude to his own presentation, where the marks made in the studio were equal to those that marked his clothes. An episode in Bacon's studio recounted in the journals of the British neo-Romantic artist Keith Vaughan demonstrates the calculated and masochistic quality of appearance that Bacon sought:

I was in his studio one day and he came in with a suit which had just come from the cleaners. He laid it down on a large table in the middle of the room which was thick with paint, cotton wool, bits of dirty paper. He laid the suit down on the top and said he had to go out for a moment. As the suit had just come from the cleaners I picked it up and put it on a hanger and hung it out of the way by the wall. My only reason for doing this is I thought it would be helpful – a small thing – but something that he was incapable of doing for himself. Directly he came back into the room, without saying a word, he went over to the wall, took the suit down and laid it again in the paint on the table. I felt absolutely shattered, as though my personality had been wiped out.[9]

In this instance, a suit is only right for the artist to wear when it bears the traces of his activity, even though he may not have been wearing it whilst painting. It is intended to construe dishevelment or a disregard for the formalities of appearance; but it is also a demonstration of the artist impregnating his dress with the materiality of his studio. The chaos of Bacon's studio was often thought of as his 'mental compost', a literal interpretation of the chaos of the modern condition made material. The wearing of the suit is therefore a signifying practice for his studio and his craft when outside its confines.

The dishevelled clutter of Bacon's studio was also to become his means of depicting the textures of male dress on canvas. As the artist recalled,

that early painting in the Tate Gallery of Eric Hall in which his suit looks immaculate is painted with dust. Actually there is no paint at all on the suit apart from a very thin grey wash on which I put dust from the floor . . . But pure dust is the perfect colour for a grey suit.[10]

In his alchemy, the material manifestation of the unkempt and idle is transformed into the even material of conformity and purpose: from dust that had settled to a surface of sedentary authority. Yet to render modernity in dress through dust is perhaps to inject human mortality

Francis Bacon in a London street, 1970.

into an object that has the ability to survive its owner whose measurement it is defined by.

Bacon worked in his studio early, rising each morning at six with a searing hangover that roused him into intensive bouts of painting at the ever-single canvas until midday approached and he began his cosmetic preparations for the day ahead. His grooming habits were by and large formed from the ingenuity forced by wartime restrictions on cosmetics and the tricks of music-hall performers employed on stage to enable projection. It was a style of latent effeminacy overpowered by the application of an all-over effect intended for darkened corners and subdued light. Painted as a performer of the street, he presented himself not as theatrical, but as conscious of the artifice of his own appearance. Bacon's preparations bled from the solitary activities of the morning, a developed synthesis between the techniques for a painted face and a painted portrait. The campness of appearing as a likeness did not escape conversation: Bacon was fond of recounting that Cowan Dobson, a London society painter of the time, liked to refer to his wife as 'the most painted woman in London'.

The art biographer John Richardson has written on the amalgamation of brushstrokes for make-up and for pictures that Bacon innovated, so that he often practised on his own face with Max Factor pancake make-up before applying those self-same brushstrokes in paint on canvas for a painted face. The effect of the surface on these brushstrokes, be it skin or canvas, would also be matched, so that a four-day-old stubble was discovered to give the same resistance and cover as the reverse side of canvas that Bacon always used. If we think about this in relation to the idea of the dress rehearsal before the performance, we can appreciate that the painting of faces by the artist was predicated by the painting of the artist's own face.

This suggests that the mask of the modern condition depicted in his paintings was based on the mask of his own appearance in the metropolis. His paintings not only reflect the interiority of experience (using the details of the modern interior), but also allude to the experience of performativity in the city (using the details of appearance). Bacon was acutely aware of the centrality of the metropolis to the modern condition; he always affected heavier make-up whenever he travelled further out of town, as if to demonstrate forcefully the purposefulness of projection across distances – a skill of *fin-de-siècle* music-hall artists. The artist Michael Wishart once observed Bacon's preparations when in Monte Carlo:

> He applied the basic foundation with lightening dexterity born of long practice. He was even more careful, even sparing with the rouge. For his hair he had a selection of Kiwi boot polishes in various browns. He blended them on the back of his hand, selecting a tone appropriate for the particular evening, and brushed them through his abundant hair with a shoe brush. He polished his teeth with Vim. He looked remarkably young even before his alchemy.[11]

The strange use of household cleaning materials for cosmetic purposes is all the more noticeable as Wishart makes no bones about their use; rather, he concentrates on the conviction of their artistic application. In essence, it was the way they were carried off, rather than the unorthodoxy of the materials, that contributed to Bacon's personal mystique.

The difference between South Kensington and Soho is the axis that informs Bacon's movements in the city. In South Kensington we find the historical status of the artist's studio, the weight of tradition in the museological Albertropolis, the leafy environs of Edwardian splendour, which all set the ensuing depravity of Soho into such delicious contrast. Bacon was fond of these settings, enabling him to frame his activities in a style as mannered as the large gilded frames and excessive glazing that contained his paintings. When expressing his liking for the colour of blood, he did so by saying 'you've only got to look into a butcher's shop like Harrods' Food Hall',[12] confirming the richness of the colour as being necessarily informed by its setting and its sense of Edwardian luxury. Such privileged carcasses were to become the props that supported the artist's portrait by John Deakin for an article in British *Vogue*, celebrating Bacon's solo exhibition at the Institute of Contemporary Arts in 1955.

John Deakin, *Portrait of Francis Bacon*, c. 1955, photograph.

Many popular historians recount that Soho life consisted of a colourful range of literary and artistic characters; they obscure a more populist notion of Soho from the period as a fearful place of gangland violence with razors, cocaine trafficking and madames strangled by silk stockings. Soho quickly bred a reputation as a temporary escape from the reality of austerity in London in the early 1950s with its rich network of watering holes, restaurants, immigrant catering establishments, drinking clubs and illicit dens. What was on offer often included the peddling of contraband goods from racketeering created by rationing.

The Spiv is a criminal character wholly associated with the area who influenced the artistic style position in question. An early-published mention of this character appears in Stanley Jackson's *Indiscreet Guide to Soho* of 1946, where:

> All over Soho you will see 'spivs' . . . Your spiv is always a snappy dresser. His jacket is a long bum-warmer, hand stitched, with the lapels generously wide. He is tailored in little back rooms where they stick a bit on the bill in lieu of coupons. His collar-attached shirts are pseudo-American and bought in the Charing Cross Road or the Edgware Road. He wears little hats with curly brims which show off his patent leather hair underneath. He likes to go to a barber shop every day for his shave, hot towels and hair brush. If there is a manicurist and a shoe-shine boy in the place he goes through all the motions of being a 'big-shot.' He puts out his hand and talks from the side of his mouth to the manicurist who gets the full blast of the 'sparkler' on his finger. None of your cheap hosiery for the spiv. While his shoes are being shined he studies his long silk socks with the quiet satisfaction of a man who has made good.[13]

The ostentatious flaunting of stylistic details in dress and a heightened interest in masculine grooming were for many causes for concern. Not only did it signal a swiftly generated wealth based on immoral means but also a posturing and interest in fanciful (and forbidden) things. As such, it was in keeping with post-war sensitivities to foreign influences and effete mannerisms informing youth formations and style positions. Tailor & Cutter noted in its leader column in 1947 that from the windows of their Gerrard Street offices they had observed that the Spiv

Francis Bacon from behind at a private view wearing a leather trench-coat, 1968.

is found in great packs around the districts of Soho and the Charing Cross Road. And to us, the Spiv's danger lies in the fact that his appearance really interests him. And that he is, to use the Spiv vernacular, ' . . . all abaht on fashion'.

This sense of style being uncontained, unbounded by institution or workplace, gives sense to Tailor & Cutter's fear at its onslaught:

He is a vulgarian and to him, music only means jazz, colour means scarlets and yellows, talking means cursing, eating means gorging, drinking means soaking and dressing means fantastic exhibitionism . . . And that is why we should be at great pains to exterminate him. For the Spiv is recruiting rapidly and is quickly becoming the backbone of the nation – that softer, more rounded and lower portion of the backbone that invariably gets kicked.[14]

To sum up the phenomenon as the arse-end of the national backbone is particular for the way it laces the image as being unmasculine, perhaps lightly asserting that the Spiv's manor was also playground to a high proportion of homosexual men. The references to suiting in cloth and colour substantiate an interest in the American drape model of suiting popularized on the Charing Cross Road by Cecil Gee; the 'little back rooms' pay reference to the presence of Jewish tailors in Soho, often from the East End, who paved the way for cheap suiting, tailoring and alterations for the soon-to-emerge demand for youth clothing that a traditional tailor would balk at. Although perhaps it is his vulgarity in the 'cursing', 'gorging' and 'soaking' that allies him so with the likes of Bacon and his cohorts. If we think about a figure such as George Melly, with his predilection for jazz, coloured zoot suits and Surrealism, it makes him an exemplary illustration of the artistic appropriation of this style.

Indeed, the tensions that pulled at the perception of the traditional Englishman and his suit in the period form useful measures for how we situate the dress of Bacon and his social circle. In the newly identified spheres of leisure for the young in the city, a difference was asserted between 'casual' and 'relaxed' dress, an intentional code of slovenliness that held its own form of associations. Many saw it as a code of casualness that was a sartorial response to the after-effects of war, underlined by the use of army surplus and second-hand clothing by persons wishing to strike the pose of a survivor.

The poet Dylan Thomas enshrined this new style position by famously addressing a fellow Fitzrovian drinker and writer, Julian Maclaren Ross: 'Fucking Dandy. Flourishing that stick. Why don't you try and look more sordid. Sordidness boy, that's the thing.'[15] The etymology of the word *sordid* derives from the French *sordide*, from the Latin *sordere* meaning 'be dirty', thus implying that sordidness can be both an internal and an external attribute. Simon Roberts's essay on Fitzrovia, a bohemian enclave to the north of Soho and possessing an artistic and literary community that eventually bled south, goes some way to culturally mapping this topographical area:

> Sordidness amounted not just to prowling, bleary-eyed and red-nosed, around Fitzrovia's narrow enclaves in shabby tweeds. Sordidness was the nearest Fitzrovia came to a collective aesthetic, whether in consciously aping Thomas' bad boy behaviour or as a reaction against Audenesque intellectualism and the refined, sherry-sipping posturings of the 'Bloomsberries'. Fitzrovia lay gutter-side of Gower Street and those who rolled through it espoused unruly causes – the Spanish Republic, Surrealism – and mixed with dubious company. Spivs and tarts were fixtures in the Wheatsheaf and the Marquess long before they became known as 'poets' pubs'.[16]

The dubious company found in this area and the swift manner in which they led south to Soho in the mid-1940s was also mapped out by Stanley Jackson, who wrote in his guide to Soho of 1946 that 'one has only to take a short walk from Great Windmill Street to Charing Cross Road via Old Compton Street to see fifty faces that would fit into the "Police Gazette" with no trouble at all'.[17] Jackson was reporting on the amount of undesirables, bohemian or not, to be found in the streets that lead from Fitzrovia to Soho, but his belief in these faces taking kindly to the techniques of a police photographer runs concurrent with the unlikely ideals held by two fashion photographers, Peter Rose Pulham and John Deakin.

Pulham was a photographer for *Harper's Bazaar* in London from 1932 to 1937, when he left for Paris to follow Surrealism. On his return to London in 1943 he continued with his photography and gave a number of notable lectures; his talk on BBC radio in 1952 was thought by Bacon to be the best thing he had ever heard on the reproductive medium. In a debate at the Institute of Contemporary Arts in the same year, Pulham defined the possibilities of post-war photography:

> Emotional and haphazard chance are the best conditions for good photography. The perfect photo is of a national calamity, when the camera is knocked out of the photographer's hand, develops itself in the gutter and is immediately published in the newspapers where its impact as a smudged image is immediate. Afterwards, the negative is stored in the police archives.[18]

Pulham's catastrophic, but also ideal conditions for taking photographs are best illustrated by his contemporary Deakin, who is now remembered mostly for photographing a great many of these Soho faces. Deakin was a drinking acquaintance of Bacon who worked at various stages as a documentary photographer for *Picture Post*, as a portrait and fashion photographer for British *Vogue*, and as a photographer who made preparatory studies of subjects for Bacon's paintings.

Deakin's photographic style was motivated by a pictorial realism so acute as to almost harm his subjects. His stark, unflinching results were often compared to police mug-shots in their quality of detail and harshness of light. Deakin claimed that in 'being fatally drawn to the human race, what I want when I photograph is to make a revelation about it. So my sitters turn into victims.' He victimized them by rendering faithfully every pore and crevice with an unkind eye, 'deforming them into [an] appearance' that spoke of age, experience, wear and tear as metropolitan subjects enduring but celebrating existence.

Undated photograph of Peter Rose Pulham. On the back is written 'Peter refusing a fashion sitting'.

While not appearing sordid, his subjects almost always appeared worn-in, possessed of a latent criminality. Bacon often said that being homosexual was much more interesting when it was illegal; this notion of deviancy, so aligned to the artist's formulation of appearance, holds particular resonance for Deakin's own photographic style and how it became sourced by Bacon's own eye for his paintings. The rarely seen publication of Deakin's topographical work, *London Today* (1949), presents a record of London awaiting post-war reconstruction and conscious of her embattled looks. An unattributed foreword states:

John Deakin, *Self-portrait*, 1960, photograph.

some cities are immediately photogenic, but London at first, is
camera shy . . . It takes time to realise that this city is a prime
example of beauty being more than skin-deep. For you can live
in London half a lifetime and still know only part of it: to explore
it is like getting on intimate terms with a difficult person – there
are rebuffs before the secrets, the true landmarks are gradually
revealed.[19]

Here, a case is made for a London that reveals itself only part by part,
over the passage of time. The temporal quality is further emphasized by
the insistence that 'perhaps what matters more than these in London is
the time and temper of the day'. In the photographs themselves this is
revealed in the foggy, slightly ethereal quality of some of the images
taken near the river; reminiscent of Brassaï's and Eugène Atget's photography of Paris at night, the stillness making them look, as Walter
Benjamin commented, like the scenes of crimes. But perhaps most of
all, it is Deakin's quest for patina, the marks of age, that qualify his
approach. In recording the dirt of the city, where the fascias of buildings are rendered by the rain-soaked incrustation of soot, he reveals an
identity formed by the *chiaroscuro* of grime – as particular to its age as
Gustave Doré's engravings of blackened London were to the nineteenth
century. In doing so, Deakin posits the appearance of the city as being
not unlike the soiled style of Dylan Thomas. A sordid appearance ravaged by the exigencies of war but ascribable to a post-war condition of
being, signified by the presence of patina. It presents the sordidness
of grime as an essential part of visual language pertaining to the streets
of London.

John Deakin's own style of dress, here, is a good case in question. As
one of the Soho characters that Daniel Farson happened upon on his
first visit to the French House on Dean Street in the spring of 1951, he
merits a full description:

One man made an entrance with the gait of a midget wrestler
and stood so close that I was struck by the details of his appearance, curiously dishevelled as if he had been rescued at sea and

fitted out in clothes donated by the crew: paint-smeared blue jeans whose zip was half-open, and a thick white polo-neck sweater now grey with age, on which blood had fallen from the ridge of congealed gore behind his ear. On top he wore a British officer's 'warm', a tattered sheepskin overcoat which was a graveyard of nostalgic wine stains and cigarette burns as if he had fallen asleep on it countless nights.[20]

Here we have an outfit that makes many claims. The sheepskin overcoat possesses a hide patterned with marks of the night. The paint-splattered jeans suggest an artistic career of uninhibited but masterful mark-making, while the weeping gash that marks his jumper sullies this with incompetence, aided by a half-opened fly. The outfit is all the more remarkable when we consider that at this time he was a house photographer for *Vogue* magazine, a world of mannered decorum that was wholly different.

To further this idea I would like to turn to *Man about Town*, 'the magazine for the gay dog' launched by Tailor & Cutter in 1955. Its intended role was to respond to the expanded potential of menswear in the post-war period through the guise of a carefree and debonair guide to being the modern man about town. As an ideal, it was wrought between upholding traditional values and dispensing cautioned advice on modern quandaries of style and manners when they arose. An article from the second issue 'Are You a Shmoe?' began a hotly contested issue concerning the new identification of a type of man unable to follow accepted standards of gentlemanly, metropolitan dress. The notion that he was 'behind the times', more than middle-aged and probably suburban, aided the filling-in of the character:

At the moment a shmoe favours wide trousers. When wide trousers come back he will be getting reacquainted with narrow trousers. In the meantime he wears a Homberg hat with a raglan overcoat, a stiff detached or even a tabbed collar with a sports jacket and a Duffel coat for all town occasions. The shmoe keeps his small change in a purse. Shmoes always have trouble shaving.

Consequently a shmoe usually has little pieces of cotton wool or cigarette paper sticking to tiny wounds underneath his chin. The clotted shmoe doesn't even bother to staunch the flow – he has blobs of congealed gore to mark where the razor dragged.[21]

The strong affinity between this description and that of John Deakin suggests that these recognizable foibles had the potential to be employed and deployed by artists keen to reject the prevailing codes of masculinity. It was, in a sense, a form of assertion through inversion. Deakin never affected the boot polish and make-up of Bacon, but his dishevelled grooming and the wine stains and fag burns were just as well rehearsed, just as well projected. The French sociologist Pierre Bordieu later identified this practice among artists as 'a sort of practical demonstration of emptiness of the values and powers it pursues'. For Bacon and his cohorts, it amounted to a convulsive masquerade. Their agitation of appearance became the source material for the accoutrements featured in Bacon's figurative works, their means to condemn the figure of the man about town and the fuel for their effete laughter when out in Soho.

End-paper illustration by Malcolm English from Tom Salter, *Carnaby Street* (1970).

CHAPTER FIVE

Remaining in Soho, but shifting slightly towards the western side, just before Regent Street leads us to a street that was responsible for awakening men to the possibilities of consuming a rapidity of style changes, at a pace that exceeded the seasonal turn of ladies' fashions. Carnaby Street became synonymous with a masculine form of colourful peacockery not seen since the early nineteenth century and made a spectacle of men being self-conscious in their consumption of fashion. It was a heightened sense of masculinity that, unlike the sluggishness and smears of the artistic dress discussed in the last chapter, was neat to the point of polish and was overly alert. Rather than using dress as a form of reserve from the pace of the city, it consumed dress at a rate that beat with the city; you could hear it in how fast they chewed gum, or in the heartbeats of many with purple dye still on their tongues.

In artistic terms, this signalled a disregard for existential gravitas and a move towards a delight in the ephemerality of popular culture. It was the work of a generation who embraced Harold Macmillan's slogan 'You've never had it so good' through personal investment in entrepreneurship. What is interesting is how this new development in menswear was produced in an area virtually indistinct from the ones walked by Bacon and his cohort – the shared characteristic being the transgressive and progressive charge of homosexual dress.

To articulate this difference through the socializing spaces of Soho, it would be the difference between The Colony Room drinking club on Dean Street, which was frequented by Bacon and presided over by Muriel Belcher, and the Il Duce coffee bar on D'Arblay Street run by Peter Burton. While both were havens for homosexual men, the first favoured suiting, waspish conversation and large measures, while the second favoured casual separates, belting Tamla Motown and small cups of coffee produced from a Gaggia machine. They are a testament to the cultural overlays that London is able to contain across the span of a few streets. As we shall see, the historical sedimentation of gay culture in Soho was fundamental to the deployment of this new shift in fashionable clothing for men.

The persistence of the 'man about town' as a construct continued to pervade the London of the 1950s, his movements defined in the magazine of the same name by the thoroughfares of Piccadilly and Regent Street that contained the theatre restaurants, men's outfitters, cocktail bars and travel agents that regularly placed advertisements in the expectation of his patronage. Although he would partake in activities that might be considered 'the fashion', the idea of his sartorial choices being defined purely by this concept was a challenge to more than his masculinity. The 'man about town' knew that the difference between ladies' clothes and men's dress was largely in the pace of their change. The measured and minimal increments of change in a man's suit was a reassurance that was to be closely guarded, an armour that afforded a dismissive view of faddishness and offered comfort in its very rigidity. And yet, it is recognized that in the post-war period British men began to participate more in the experience of shopping. With the aid of the advertising, marketing and retailing industries, masculine consumption not only increased, but was also subject to the creation of new practices of shopping.

In the case of buying clothes, these new practices were often moulded by entrepreneurs keen to fashion distinctive new style positions for young men. In turn, this created a situation in which these style positions were understood through their consumption: by the space, place and location of the sale. This example charts a relationship between Carnaby Street, a London street transformed into a shopping destination of landmark status, and John Stephen, the entrepreneur credited for changing not only the street but also the notion of menswear. It extrapolates the distinctions between retailer, consumer and retail area from a moment of social history that remains heavily mythologized. By doing this I want to suggest that shops and shopping areas can be held responsible for the creation of style positions for men, and that these identities are strongly bound to a popular understanding of these spaces, even to the point of disadvantage.

John Stephen is credited with the title 'King of Carnaby Street' for his swift commercial assault on dressing the modern male youth of London in the 1960s. He was largely responsible for transforming a low-rent street of tobacconists into the central site for the consumption

John Stephen,
1968.

Tearsheet from *Man's World*, 1961, showing Neil Christian in a John Stephen shirt.

of 'Swinging London'. What is particular to this reputation is the accelerated density of Stephen's expansion. His business evolved from a single shop in 1957 to 22 in Greater London (9 of these with Carnaby Street addresses) by 1966. By 1975, the year that The John Stephen of London Group was wound up, the company had significantly expanded, employing 400 staff, with 2 factories, a design team, publicity department and 30 shops in Europe and the USA.

In British youth subcultural history, Stephen has earned a special place for offering an accelerated range of choice to young men eager for difference, and for constructing spaces conducive to shopping and social interaction. Pictorial evidence confirms how the self-awareness of this consumption went beyond the confines of the shop fittings and was played out in a burgeoning street culture ripe for media attention.

Within a history of post-war British men's dress, John Stephen appears as a symbol of 'modernist' aspirations in appearances formulated into mod uniform for sale. Although not the first to understand the post-war potential for 'drag' or casual separates, Stephen took Bill Green's example (Green was the owner of Vince's Man's Shop, where he had formerly worked as a salesman) but applied a greater degree of business acumen so that Vince's largely homoerotic style was filtered for mass consumption. However, post-1965 the business was obscured by the rise of Chelsea bohemianism and the increasing commercial gluttony of Carnaby Street, which dulled its edge. While 'authentic' beginnings are always of greater historical interest than commercial excess, Stephen deserves a fuller definition of his business and its contribution to men's dress in London.

The lack of historical clarity is in large part due to the mythology of 'Swinging London' as a concept, usually credited to *Time* magazine in

Interior of a John Stephen store with a tie display using branches, 1967.

1966 but actually first discussed by the American John Crosby in the *Daily Telegraph* colour supplement a year earlier.[1] The whimsical tone of the article and the flippancy of the journalist who claimed, among many other things, that London girls take to sex 'as if it's candy', helped to define not only Swinging London but also the style in which it was reported. The cultural historian Jonathan Green's commentary on Crosby's interpretation of fashion retailers and designers is particularly apt:

> Mary Quant 'and a bunch of other pretty Chelsea Birds' have revolutionised fashion; Julie Christie gets her name check, as do Bailey and 'Terry' Donovan and Carnaby Street retailer John Stephen, obligatory poles on the make, although when it comes to fashion Crosby is soon out of Carnaby Street and even the King's Road, and heading back to the classier world of Blades, where Rupert Lycett Green, the very model of a youthful upper-class dandy, set up to dress his peers.[2]

Crosby is described as a kind of whirling *flâneur*, crossing class distinctions and metropolitan zones in a style wholly derived from the English aristocracy's knack for 'mixing it' at social occasions. The term refers to the inclusion of artistic, bohemian and creative individuals who existed outside upper-class society, but who were invited to social events to add what was then considered excitement and local colour. The idea of 'mixing it' was a strong catalyst to American onlookers, as Andrea Adam, journalist at *Time* magazine, confirmed when recounting the 'Swinging London' edition of 1966: 'We perceived a classlessness coming from the aristocracy, who were very heavily involved too, that we found very attractive. People seemed easy-going about their titles.'[3] The laissez-faire attitude was also to be reflected in the reporting, where specificity and detail were often bleached by the reconfigured, journalistic narrative (lacing the term 'mixing it' with a very different connotation). It is worth noting here that it was the very different 'take' on the city that these articles made that helped Britons see London afresh, such was the allure of the American aesthetic.

This is further ramified by Christopher Booker's observation in his critique of British society in the period that in 1958 the upper-class and working-class young were meeting 'in the new "classless" middle ground of jeans and modern jazz, of "hip" and "cool", of casual Americanised clothes and casual Americanised speech that foreshadowed the pop culture to come'.[4] This is of crucial importance to the formulation of the 'New Establishment' as defined by the work of David Bailey: not only to foreground origins of terms such as 'cool', but also to set a notion of 'mixing it' within the consumption of clothing and style.

It is generally accepted by historians such as Green that Bailey's two publications of the 1960s are testaments to those who constituted this scene. His role in deciding who 'was' and who 'wasn't' in largely defines those remembered for posterity. The first, *Bailey's Box of Pin-Ups* (1965), gave conceptual meaning to the newly found 'in crowd'. Inside a box lay assorted captioned pictures of individuals that aimed to capture 'the ephemeral glamour' of the transitory scene. This was then laid to rest with *Goodbye, Amen to All That: A Saraband for the Sixties* (1969), a book of many more portraits and a text by Peter Evans.

Bailey's portraiture helped the foundation of the New Establishment by privileging youth, vitality and creativity as an expression of classlessness that rejected the stuffiness of convention. This combination was regularly mixed and applied by the new media titles such as *Queen, Man about Town* and the *Sunday Times Magazine*, moving beyond the mere reporting of the said individuals towards a worded formula that could equate with a shift in society. It is the very closeness of this formula to the photographic style developed by Bailey that inverts it back to something that was only mediated, something that barely existed. It makes the stark black and whites seem like notoriety in the papers, the pores of the skin a stark reality, the flat backdrop colour framing the portraits as unreal and 'flat as a magazine page'. This in turn served to gloss the specificity of the individual, so that they reverberated collectively only as a series of images.

John Stephen was easily allied to this kind of treatment: the clipped story following his portrait in *Goodbye, Amen to All That* tells of the boy who worked in the menswear department of the Glasgow Co-op and then moved to London, where he worked double shifts to raise the money to open his first store, which became 'the boom that made the most famous fashion carnival in the world: Carnaby Street'. Accelerated transformation is the central motif to the definition and it became synonymous with the designer. The combination of the young male on the periphery and metropolitan success was central to John Stephen's appeal and to the consumption of his clothes by suburban boys. What is interesting is how this definition marked Stephen's reputation; how the looseness in the construction of the prerequisites and their application were eventually to mark him as fixed and essentially different from others in the field of menswear.

John Stephen inherited his initial custom from his previous employer, Bill Green. Green was a physique photographer who had branched into retailing separates on the back of a success found in selling unusually coloured men's briefs. Catering largely to butch gay trade (the Marsham Street Baths were local, as was the Palladium Theatre), Vince's sold a range of Continental styles: American-imported blue denim jeans, black turtlenecks reputedly from the Left Bank, Italianate hipster-cut trousers and Greek fishing caps. The unusual items, often fashioned in unconventional fabrics, began to attract select custom, and celebrated individuals gradually began to patronize the shop.

John Stephen took Vince's as a model for his shop, but realized that the key to transforming the scale of the operation was to involve heterosexual young men, who would assist in the translation and diffusion of what was essentially homosexual dress into the fashion mainstream as a modern and optimistic trend, unbounded by sexual orientation. This was largely achieved by undercutting Vince's market, since Stephen realized that most teenagers would be unable to afford to shop there.

Stephen was to take advantage of the techniques of advertising 'drag' goods through veiled terms – often a combination of innocuous model poses and a suggestively worded narrative in the underground gay press – translating the style for an emerging media that served the teenage consumer market. Instead of nameless models, Stephen used his famous clientele; instead of innuendo, information was typed on the back of the press photograph on the star's latest pursuits.

Much of this was secured by Mike McGrath, a pop-group photographer and women's magazine journalist who helped to cement Stephen's constant good relations with the media. Their first success was a photograph in 1962 of the British boxing hope Billy Walker, dressed in tight-fitting slacks and a striped matelot shirt (modelling with a young Caroline Neville). The photograph was blown up and used as a backdrop to the window displays in all the shops. In terms of the codes of window display for men's shops, it was revolutionary to see a heterosexual boxer of considerable repute modelling what was considered 'drag' clothing.

Music was established as an active component of the shops, as was an attention to detail in window display and interior design. John Stephen was one of the first to identify these elements as a factor in encouraging men to shop for pleasure, and assigned the tasks to an in-house display artist, Anthony Myers, typical of the new cachet of professions previously thought of as down at heel.

Inside the initial spaces Scandinavian-style blond slatted false ceilings hung next to fine Italianate ironwork arches, while black-and-white vinyl tiles hinted at Venetian stone floors. Each element was presented not in terms of an overall design, but as a series of applied effects reminiscent of those used in stage design. Blown-up photographs of Piranesi's graphic works were employed for their strong, structural and masculine decorative associations – a visual style that nodded to classical beauty while referencing the modern Italianate vogue in its rendering.

At this point, the Continentally derived style was imported in much the same way as the casual separates. They were recognized as lexicons of travel, leisure and unconventional sophistication and were used to frame the new masculine experience of shopping for clothes as a participatory act. More interestingly, they helped to mask the movement of the mirror from the changing room to the shop floor. Mirror walls were often the main feature of the designed interior, not only for the customer's reflection but also to give the illusion of space in what were cramped retail settings. The disguise of what was essentially a communal mirror into an aspect of the interior design meant that self-awareness was no longer an isolated experience, but something played out in a context that architecturally echoed the street.

The strong recognition of change in the London landscape of the 1960s was a motivational factor in the belief in accelerated progress. More than any other material, the architectural use of the glass curtain became symbolic of self-awareness both in its transparency and in its ability to reflect. The mimicking of this in the use of plate mirror in shop design could be construed as parody, but at this point parody was restrained, almost pared-down – suggestive of *naïveté*. For parody was formulated not in the interior, or in dress, but in window display.

The example of the artist Robyn Denny's mural of 1959 for Austin Reed's flagship store in Regent Street is particularly relevant here because it was commissioned in response to the growing threat of nearby Carnaby Street and its youth styles to middle-market menswear, well represented in Regent Street. (It was not until 1961 that John Stephen opened the first 'official' boutique for men on Regent Street.) Denny was a recently graduated painter from the Royal College of Art, and his brief was to engage the new consumer market and modernize the company image by 'adopting the signs of metropolitan novelty'. His

Robyn Denny, *'GREAT, BIG, WIDE, BIGGEST!'* mural, 1959, oil on board.

mural was a red, white and blue typographic collage of words that
screamed the frenetic jargon of advertising and celebrated London as
'GREAT, BIG, WIDE, BIGGEST!'

To evaluate how this impacted upon a sense of the marketing and
design of Swinging London, one should consider the design as reorder-
ing the visual grammar of a national symbol to present an understanding of the metropolitan landscape as fractured and complex. The Austin
Reed mural took the traditional forms of advertising and display that
promoted London and represented them to the discerning, knowledge-
able metropolitan consumer. It was concerned with reconfiguring the
known cultural landscape with irreverence in a slightly self-congratula-
tory manner. Most importantly, it was for the home market – not for
the tourist gaze. In combination, the language of advertising London
and the Union Jack flag became visual emblems of a new London,
hijacked and interpreted in less imaginistic ways for window display.
This is the crux: without the artistic intervention the emblems became
merely representative; without graphic distortion they were recognizable, guiding tourist experience rather than reformulating it.

The importance of the role of window display for Swinging London
was based not in the capital, but in America with the concurrent rise of
Beatlemania. (It is curious that one of the Beatles' first London photo-
sessions in 1963 was in front of the Austin Reed mural.) The marketed
imagery of the Beatles in America was largely complemented by the traditional icons of tourist London: Bobbie hats, traffic signs, Union Jacks,
Trooping the Colour. The literal quality of their presentation was in order
for American eyes to understand them. The obviousness of the reproduction of the symbols of the street was intended to ease the tourists'
passage, but what they also succeeded in doing was confusing them.

It is at this point that the American misunderstanding of the word
'mod' becomes particularly poignant. In taking it to mean 'modern' they
ascribed it to anything new coming out of London, including elements
as arbitrary as Lord Snowdon, Carnaby Street, restaurants, Mary Quant,
nightclubs and Vidal Sassoon. Although all were elements of a social and
cultural framework developing around London, they bore no relation to
the set of consumers who frequented John Stephen and defined a sub-

Tearsheet from *Titbits*, 1 January 1966.

SYLVIA LAMOND takes a

CATHY McGOWAN, of television, said to John Stephen, of Carnaby Street: "You shouldn't run a Rolls-Royce, you know, John.

"You'll ruin your image. You're letting down your young public."

In his soft, clipped Glaswegian voice, John Stephen said to me:

"Cathy McGowan is a very opinionated gir-r-rl. I canna think of anything when I see her, but her seams. Terrible seams. One shoulder up here . . . one down here. But she's not one to listen, so I save m'breath."

John Stephen is an opinionated person himself. At 29, he has the right to be.

He is the best-known name in men's wear—at the brighter end of the trade. He has been called the "Million Pound Mod" and he has made clothes for the

There's taped music and photographed pin-up boys at Trecamp, John Stephen's fashion shop for girls in Carnaby Street, London. This checked wool mini-skirt costs 59s 6d, the skinny sweater 35s and the black and white cloche hat 26s 6d

cultural identity. In invention becoming appearance, the coded qualities of the mods' patterns of consumption were appropriated and diluted into a surface that could be applied, like a veneer, to a range of other phenomena. It is the American media's process of turning subcultural modes of consumption, dress and behaviour into a model for reporting on aspects of metropolitan creativity and living that is particularly pertinent. The opening of John Stephen's first shop for girls, Trecamp, prompted an article in the *New York Herald Tribune*:

It's Trecamp – even if the salesgirls don't know what that means. You can't blame them too much either, Trecamp being a combination of très (French for very) and camp (American for, well, camp) … Inside the changing rooms are not the usual mirrors, but three blow-up, life size pictures of boys. Handsome boys, who are what's more, in various states of undress. One, a blond Adonis type (and an art student in real life), is bare-chested and is sliding down his trunks zipper (which, however, is placed sideways) while giving you a full, toothy smile. In the second sitting room, there is a slightly built and what the English call sweet-looking boy, in trunks again and taking off – no, not his trunks – but his shirt, and looking at you in a sort of sad and deadpan way. The boy is the lead singer in a new beat group called 'The Carnaby'.[5]

Trecamp was Stephen's response to the ever-growing demand for his clothes by women who favoured the casual, androgynous styles. What is relevant is how the shop's interior decoration parodied others in the street catering to men, and in doing so became a cause for concern for the American journalist – much horrified by Anthony Myer's proclamation that the mannequins in the window display were 'bisexual. Their bosoms and wigs come off – and we can use them in the boy's stores too.' The interchangeable nature of the look was indicative of a diluted formula and an economy of means, rather than any attempt at a sexual revolution in window display that the article was keen to warrant. Still, the interior decoration made the news on the other side of the Atlantic.

The French fashion historian Farid Chenoune identifies the three stages of mod (both as a youth subculture and a style of dress) as 'modernist' between 1958 and 1961, 'mod' between 1961 and 1963, and 'modest' (referring to those on tight budgets and of-a-pack mentality) between 1963 and 1966. The modernists, named for their liking of modern as opposed to traditional jazz, derived pleasure from the consumption of rarefied commodities including imported black vinyl, imported white Ivy-League shirts, tailor-made mohair and silk suits, and custom-made shoes. With a quickly established code of narcissism,

Mod customers dress well, but the tailors are just as smart: at making money

Carnaby Street shoppers wear their hair long — and cut a dash with their clothes

I N London, it is the nearest thing to a Latin carnival you will see: throngs of young men, elegantly dressed in flamboyant colours, elbowing each other to press their noses against the shop windows. And it all happens in one rather dingy side-street.

This is Carnaby Street, Soho, a thimble's throw from Savile Row.

Like Savile Row, it is a street of tailors, a centre of high fashion, the place where good taste is decided. So far as Britain's Mods are concerned, anyway.

From all over the country, they flock there every Saturday to buy their silken wool sweaters (£4), elastic-grip shoes (£6), mohair trousers (£9) and two-tone suede jackets with Prussian collars (£21).

And while their money flows over the counter, one man is already calculating what will be "in" when those pop fashions are "out."

They call him the King of Carnaby Street: John Stephen, a 27-year-old Scot with a talent for keeping tuned in to the youngsters' tastes.

Only eight years ago, he was a shop assistant with a spare-time job in a snack-bar to boost his savings. Now he owns a chain of 18 Mod shops, including one in Carnaby Street, and casually remarks:

"Any year now I'll be a millionaire."

Unlike most tailors, Carnaby Street men never issue brochures. They would be out of date in a few weeks. Styles change with bewildering rapidity.

The tailors are sometimes very bewildered. Not long ago, they were puzzled by a flood of orders for white trousers. At last, they found the answer. Mods were strutting out with each leg dyed a different colour.

Carnaby Street is where most of the pop stars buy their clothes. Among its customers are the Beatles, the Dave Clark Five, Cliff Richard, Tommy Steele—and other somewhat surprising names.

Marlene Dietrich, Brigitte Bardot and Petula Clarke have shopped there. They discovered that hipster pants look good on girls as well as boys.

Today, Mod fashions mean big money. Consider John Stephen. Besides taking him close to that £1,000,000, paying for his own 14 suits, five sports jackets, four casual jackets, 24 pairs of trousers, 48 shirts and 70 ties, the youngsters' cash has also provided him with a £6,000 Rolls-Royce.

And even in a world where fashions change fast, that is one thing which is always "in" with the smart set.

Hipster pants for him can suit her, too

For a fellow, it's a big decision: is that flower-pot hat really him?

Most Mods are lads with ambition. Their dream is to own a suede and leather top-coat. Price: £34

Modism has its own rewards — like John Stephen's £6,000 Rolls

It's a man's life in the modern shopping centre . . . now that boys are pop fashion's front line

Mick Jagger and Keith Richards in John Stephen, 'Gear Street', tearsheet from *Weekend*, 17–24 June 1964.

In Carnaby Street, girls find the things they like – for their boys

From bushy top to polished toe, a perfect Mod with *all* the gear

For clothes-conscious Mods, this is heaven – row after row of hipster pants to try on

they identified the act of consumption as a self-conscious pursuit that one should spend time on and be seen partaking of. Because of this, a shop such as John Stephen's relinquished its role as an insular affair for a select clientele and became a space of commerce that engaged the street and propositioned passers-by. Thus Carnaby Street entered into its modern incarnation with a brief episode of 'authentic' goods, 'considered' consumption, 'real' street culture and undiscovered, almost illicit pleasures. Snippets of press editorials from the period include an adolescent and as yet unknown Mick Jagger and Keith Richards photographed lost in the contemplation of a purchase nestling inside a John Stephen paper bag.

The devaluing of the term mod was not isolated to America, but was becoming manifest in the clothes of the Carnaby Street boutiques. Mod clothing had always possessed an ironic stance towards established social values, parodying smartness to the point of obsessiveness. But the evolution of mod style in terms of retailing on Carnaby Street changed that. The mods gave John Stephen the fast beat of consumption that he matched; Stephen was able to supply a continual differentiated range of stock that could keep up with the weekly changes, the weekend dances and the weekly charts. The problem was in regenerating the original array of casual, separate styles.

It is generally agreed that around 1965, as with other areas of pop culture, the demand for ever-evolving newness forced a distraction from innovation and invention towards a plundering and interpretation of historical styles. This can also be understood in terms of a simplification of codes and details, often reduced down to the lowest common denominator. In terms of menswear, an obvious example would be a shift from the Union Jack jacket (as worn by The Who) to the adoption of military uniform as emblematic of a disregard for the establishment. Stephen responded to the speed of the market by adapting designs from other sources: Italy was exchanged for India, op and pop exchanged for the nostalgic and foppish.

A press photograph from September 1964 captures this approach in its infancy. It depicts John Stephen in a sharply cut suit holding one hand of a shop mannequin dressed in nineteenth-century military

John Stephen with a male model and a mannequin wearing a military dress uniform. Press photo, 1964.

uniform whose other hand is held by a model wearing thin trousers and a striped cotton kurta. Although the intention behind the image is now lost, we do know that on first coming to London Stephen worked in the military department at Moss Bros. However, to see both Indian and military influences in men's dress being brought together nearly two years before they acquired their counter-cultural connotations is indicative of a naive playing of historical and cultural styles in a bid to render difference and attract fashion.

Yet this playfulness soon became tiring when produced on a weekly basis. Thus the effect became the spectacle, rather than the consumers, or the clothes. All that remained was for the tourists to see the spectacle, and the product for sale to become the souvenir. At this point the clothing shifted from being clothing consumed by mods into modernity clothed as consumption. Surprisingly, this was echoed at the time in John Stephen's advertising. A magazine advertisement from 1968 in *Queen* depicts a group of people reading a map with the attached copy:

> Carnaby Street. When John Stephen found it twelve years ago, it was just a tiny turning tucked behind Regent Street . . . Come and see. Particularly if you're looking for Regent Street. It's tucked just behind Carnaby Street.[6]

Instead of communicating ideas about the latest men's fashions, the advertisement communicates the legacy of male fashion in post-war London, pitting the fame of Carnaby Street against the middle-market majority of Regent Street. Yet, in exchanging the image of the fashionable male for the unfashionable tourist, any sense of the original innovation is lost. This was the predicament that John Stephen actively embraced: a fame that alienated his original clientele. For even though the mods expressed themselves primarily as consumers, they were ruined by the commercialism of Carnaby Street and their intentions led them elsewhere.

In being labelled 'King of Carnaby Street' John Stephen suffered from a very particular relationship with the reputation of the street, something now tangible and not merely a media invention. By the mid-1960s the street sign had become the best-selling London tourist postcard, an attraction to rival any other. Capitalizing on the worldwide interest in Swinging London, Carnaby Street became the only tangible destination for those keen to participate in a slice of the action. To this end, the purpose of the street was to dazzle: competitors vied with each other using a cocktail of loud music, camp decor and glittery, badly made clothes.

The ephemerality of the look had become too enwrapped in the instant and the disposable, appealing far more to the needs of the day-tripper than the discerning consumer. The crass commercialism levelled at Carnaby Street was not unjustified; record marketing executives had even tried to popularize an invented dance called the Carnaby. John Stephen responded seriously by launching the Beau Brummell award for the best-dressed personality of the year.

His final riposte was to move beyond the concept of the boutique and embrace the department store. After 1966 Stephen sold all his shops outside Carnaby Street, downscaling from twenty to eight on the road he believed he had begun. Instead of gimmicks, he embraced principles. By the late 1960s the dress of youth culture had dissolved into a disarray of hippy beads, kaftans, military scarlet and a kind of Regency brocade. In addition, the innovations that the modernists had made in men's dress were having populist repercussions:

> Thousands of British fathers have been bashfully copying their son's sense of dress in an attempt to keep up with modern trends – and have knocked the bottom out of the mod market. But worse. Dad just hasn't queered the teenage pitch, he's also making a mess of himself.[7]

Stephen responded to this climate by cutting out the flamboyance and concentrate on 'fairly sober trend-conscious clothes',[8] which included the reintroduction of the three-piece suit. Flamboyance was to reassert itself in and around Savile Row, led by Michael Fish, a former assistant managing director at John Stephen who was backed by Barry Sainsbury. Michael Fish and Rupert Lycett Green distanced themselves from youth by price and the prestige of location, whereas John Stephen attempted to do this by policy. He emphasized shop design, service, colour range and choice, famously offering a shirt in 50 colours, indicating that he was interested in upgrading his customer base by dealing in a luxury product. Yet by this time London already possessed a shopping area outside Savile Row that had gained a reputation for supplying clothes with flair to the discerning male consumer.

Carnaby Street was not the only shopping area that was transformed by the emergence of the idea of Swinging London. The King's Road in Chelsea was, most famously, the setting for Mary Quant's assault on women's fashion conducted with her husband Alexander Plunket Greene from the shop Bazaar, opened in 1955. Yet the King's Road was very much more than a shopping zone; it was home not only to the 'Chelsea Set', but also had an 'ambience' drawn from the reporting of bistros and boutiques in glossy magazines. As Mary Quant recounted in her autobiography: 'Nobody has ever been able to make up his mind precisely what the "Chelsea Set" was but I think it grew out of something in the air which developed into a serious attempt to break away from the Establishment.'[9] For Quant, her youthful designs were not intended to challenge the divisions of class in dress (her clothes were supposedly bought both by the daughters of dukes and the daughters of dock workers), but were intended to emphasize the distinction between her generation and that of her mother's. The paradox was that the emphasis of the designs in making young women look like little girls (or 'dolly girls') was what made them problematic for the establishment.

Quant was a crucial figure of the 'New Aristocracy', but her inclusion was not merely for her creativity, but also for her positioning. Quant was reared in south London, identified by Booker as part of the Young (Creative) Urban Lower Class that also included John Stephen. However, because of her marriage to Eton-educated Plunket Greene and the location of her business, she was accorded alternative status. This raises questions about the possibility of class characteristics being embedded in retail areas. The possible sedimentation of upper-middle-class values residing in Chelsea as a retailing area is underlined by the presence of Terence Conran's pre-digested shopping experience *Habitat*, which opened in the King's Road in 1964, and other shops including Alice Pollock's *Quorum*, Michael Rainey's *Hung on You* and Nigel Weymouth's *Granny Takes a Trip*.

In terms of a masculine identity being reconciled with the area, this was provided by a kind of louche dandyism promoted by Christopher Gibbs, editor of *Vogue for Men*. Very much an individualist, Gibbs is credited with being the first man to sport flares in 1961 and to order flower-print shirts as early as 1964. Yet, for his innovations in masculine dress, Gibbs and his circle were traditional in their care for quality and in their wish to distance themselves from the tat of Carnaby Street.

Even though this group of individuals originally patronized Blades (run by an Etonian shopkeeper) when it was located in Dover Street (near the Savile Row area), they colonized Chelsea and Kensington for their rich and civilized connotations. By the time of the opening of Hung on You in 1965, they had begun an innovation in men's dress that started the descent into the hippy vogue for anti-taste and solidified a masculine identity in opposition to that of Carnaby Street. This is well demonstrated by an article in *Life* magazine in 1966 titled 'So Long Sad Sack', which analysed developments in men's dress in London, Paris and Chicago, but with firm emphasis on London as being central to the rejection of the staid suit:

> It all began with the teen-age 'mods' (*Life International* July 27, 1961) who spent most of their money on flamboyant clothes. Now the frills and flowers are being adopted in other strata of Britain's society . . . London's fashion revolution is not all teen-agers and pop singers in op-arty tie and thigh-high boots. A new aristocratic tailoring establishment such as Blades is being influenced by the Carnaby Street look. The Chelsea shops offer several elegant variations on the new attire such as a 1920s silent movie look and an increasingly popular Edwardian look.[10]

As a whole, the article adheres strongly to the style of American reporting discussed earlier (a good example being the statement that Blades was influenced by the Carnaby Street look). It presents two oppositional themes over two spreads, which, although possessing inaccuracies, helps to confirm the presence of two masculine style positions in London differentiated by class and location. The first presented

John Stephen with models posing around a Cadillac on Carnaby Street, The Kinks in a studio shot with the lyrics to 'Dedicated Follower of Fashion' printed underneath and Nigel Weymouth standing outside Granny Takes a Trip with Michael Chaplin (son of Charlie Chaplin). This inaccuracy (Granny Takes a Trip was decidedly Chelsea) is underlined by the copy: 'One secret of [their] success is the determination of London's young men to dress differently than their bowler-hatted elders.' In total, the layout places emphasis on vitality, solidarity, a rejection of convention and a straight-off-the-peg newness.

The second spread documents the actor David Hemmings trying on a jacket in Blades; the Duke of Bedford in his Canaletto Room; Ossie Clark, Nigel Winterbottom and Michael Williams in a Chelsea pub; and Christopher Gibbs, 'a leader of Chelsea's chic bluebloods, wear[ing] a silk and lace shirt and Renoir like hat – an overall 1900 allure'. Here, the oppositional values of privilege, tradition and order are asserted, most tellingly in Gibbs's proclamation: 'We encouraged friends to dig into their heirlooms, to wear old clothes, to turn their backs on ugliness and conformism.'

This use of old clothing as an indicator of noble descent became important as a sign of taste and status, but this was also mirrored in a wider and more accessible vogue still enshrined in the Chelsea area. Barbara Hulanicki of Biba was reported as saying:

> I love old things. Modern things are so cold. I need things that have lived. Baffling words for such a 'with it' designer . . . with everything around her so fast, so uncertain, she needs to go home to . . . the comfort of dark red wallpaper and Edwardiana. It makes her feel safe.[11]

Hulanicki's response to the maddening, modern environment by making recourse to old things was symptomatic of cultural changes unbound by location. The developing apotheosis of the Beatles towards mysticism and the influence of San Francisco's Haight-Ashbury district shifted youth culture and dress into a different direction. In terms of perception this moved from 'uppers' (a sharp, excited, amphetamine

John Stephen (second right), posing outside his shop in Carnaby Street, 1 January 1966.

thrill) to 'downers' (a loose, blissful, hashish buzz). It could also be defined as moving from the world of working-class mods to that of middle-class hippies, a gendered shift towards a more feminine style and a move in dress from a position of taste to one of anti-taste. Beyond youth culture, however, taste was being reasserted in the realms of magazine publishing and consumerism to redefine 'The New Class'.

The next move was to raise distinctions within a media phenomenon that had previously been described as classless. This was achieved by moving away from associations with youth as an indicator of vitality and embracing a rarefied, metropolitan knowledge of 'Who? Why? Where? When?'. The index pages of *Queen* displayed in tabular form the 'Yes' and 'No' answers to a range of issues such as 'Artists to have at your party', 'Discothèques', 'Bistros', 'Women's hairdressers' and 'Men's Clubs'. John Stephen's custom-built tailoring was a 'No', while Blades for

Michael Williams, Ossie Clark, Julia Cooke and Neil Winterbotham at The Salisbury pub, 1 January 1966.

'Who Do The British Look Up To?', tearsheet from *The Observer* magazine, 1 December 1968.

shirts was a 'Yes'. Swelling expressions of personal identity into what Jonathan Raban considered 'a new pornography of taste',[12] the development attracted former modernists who had become disillusioned with what their elemental identity had become aligned with. For many of them, it was the realization that newness was no longer required as a badge of modernity, and that this was replaced by the value of taste, largely effected through arbitrary changes in the value of commodities. In placing themselves as affective to these changes, they can be considered as early exponents of what we now term stylists.

Carnaby Street now required no 'special kind of city knowledge' to navigate or consume, and the attempt to transform its tired emblems into another guise of fashionability is symptomatic of Stephen's protective defence of his invention, but also ultimately of how he had lost contact with the young fashionable male who was once his customer. When being interviewed for Nik Cohn's book *Today There Are No*

Gentleman (1971) he looked out of his office window onto Carnaby Street:

> 'Who are they?' said John Stephen, smiling his sorrowful smile. 'They're nobody in particular; they're Mister Average.' One day, presumably, it was bound to collapse . . . 'The street itself may go,' said Stephen. 'The changes it made will still be there.'[13]

In 1975 John Stephen and his partner Bill Frank sold their stakes in The John Stephen of London Group and the business closed. In the following year the artist Victor Burgin created a photographic poster for fly-posting that depicted a couple embracing with the caption 'What does possession mean to you? 7% of our population own 84% of our wealth'. Burgin belonged to a new breed of politically motivated artists keen to critique advertising for its role in capitalist consumption. The style of the poster was meant to be innocuous and merely ape recognizable formats. The closeness of the layout to those of John Stephen's late advertising campaigns calls to question the shift in a business that communicated fashionability through its close relation to the style of the street to one that communicated fashionability through advertising campaigns directed at an elite minority who no longer wished to be associated with it. It implies that 'possession' clearly meant two very different things to the two different types of male consumers. For the modernists, possession was something to be played out in the street; for the stylists possession was something to secure away from the street. To the misfortune of John Stephen, possession in this context was wanted by neither Mr Average nor Mr '7%'. This confirms Green's observation about the classless revolution of which John Stephen and his business were so much a part: 'for Swinging London equality was never the point'.[14]

John Stephen in Carnaby Street, 1968.

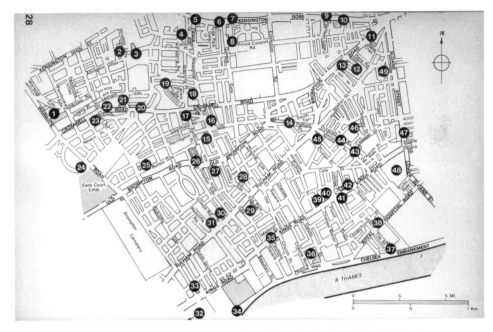

Parts of Kensington and Chelsea in a map from Christopher Booker and Candida Lycett Green, *Goodbye London: An Illustrated Guide to Threatened Buildings* (1973).

CHAPTER SIX

Leaving John Stephen in Carnaby Street (a plaque that bears his name now hangs at the southern end of the road) and drifting west back towards the King's Road along much of its length to the bend in the road that signals World's End. The supremacy of the King's Road as the shopping area for fashionable clothing for both men and women in London was undoubtedly cemented by the arrival of punk in the late 1970s. In a very simplistic sense, the tourist postcard that replaced the street sign for Carnaby Street as a symbol of a vibrant and fashionable street culture was the one that pictured 'punks' with spiky hair and leather jackets loitering on the King's Road. While this historical development is popularly accepted, a sense of how the one fed into the other from the late 1960s into early 1970s is fairly unexplored. The idea of Malcolm McLaren buying a pair of scarlet hipsters from a John Stephen store on Carnaby Street seems incredulous, but it happened. What this curious piece of information does is to give us a strange sense of connection between two distinct historical periods in London fashion: between the end of the swinging sixties and the beginning of punk – between '68 and '76. This chapter maps a connection between the idealism inscribed into these two historical dates.

In a television programme about the rise of punk written and presented by Janet Street-Porter for London Weekend Television in the late 1970s, the boutique owner Trevor Miles bemoaned the sea of flared and faded jeans that flooded the length of the King's Road in Chelsea in the mid-1970s:

> Since the last three or four years it's absolutely died a death and there's been absolutely nothing; and then there's been this amazing revival in the last eighteen months or so, and I've been doing nothing in that period of time because there's been nothing to latch on to. There's no feeling. There's no real pulse in the King's Road, which there was really, back in '67 to '71 say.[1]

As he leant over his shop counter towards the camera, illuminated by coloured tubular lighting and shielded by black Venetian blinds, Miles espoused a vision for 1977 that was not about bondage trousers and muslin shirts, but more to do with imported dark denim Fiorucci jeans and tight-fitting cap-sleeved Italian T-shirts. His fondness for the King's Road between 1967 and 1971 was due to his memories of the shop he ran at no. 430 before Malcolm McLaren took it over from him when he failed to return from an extended holiday to America in November 1971. His shop, Paradise Garage, was the first in London to import second-hand vintage denims for sale, and Osh Kosh Dungarees were sported with Hawai'ian shirts. The exterior of the shop was clad in bamboo, while the interior was painted black, with a jukebox playing loudly in the middle, selling a now wry and hollow celebration of the American aesthetic of plenty, albeit in second-hand terms. In the sole remaining photograph of the shop, Miles sits astride his hand-painted Mustang in open provocation to all those other retailers still peddling cheesecloth and corduroy as fashionably hippy.

Miles's comments about the denim-coloured sea of mediocrity that plagued retailing in the King's Road between the late 1960s and the late 1970s is also in keeping with the many cultural historians who like to celebrate the counter-cultural highpoints of the student revolts that marked the end of Swinging London in 1968 and the birth of punk in

1976, but prefer to gloss over what went on in between. The sporadic evolvement of boutiques on the King's Road and the proposed redevelopments for Oxford Street, London's busiest shopping thoroughfare, bore many indicators of the pervasive cultural themes of the period, such as retrochic, resistance, postmodernism and new realism, with an ease and speed as if they were just another set of temporary fascias to aid the sale of goods.

With his film of Oxford Street of 1969 and his opening of his first shop on the King's Road in 1971, Malcolm McLaren was one of the few to recognize at the time that these two commercial areas harnessed a possibility for shifting the cultural agenda by dressing radical ideas in the trappings of consumption. And it was fashion made and sold in London that truly reflected the cultural oscillations that spanned this period.

The cultural shorthand that is 1968 and 1976 has inscribed each date with a condensed range of historical factors. The year 1968 signals a waking from collective fantasy to reality, a sobering after a violent phase of transition that forced a crisis in consumerism, the exhaustion of pop, the death of the American dream and the fuelling of student unrest; 1976 evokes the British drought, an air of apathy and violence, the breakdown of the British infrastructure, the three-day week, the floundering of politics, the reign of high unemployment and the birth of punk.

More recently, the idealism inscribed into these dates has become a kind of byword used to support a contemporary fashionable positioning strongly defined by dress (the contemporary men's clothing label '6876' being the most literal example). The magazine *Crash!* confirmed this in 1999 as the 'Prada Meinhof' principle, a theory of contemporary malaise where fashion borrows its creditability from the visual culture of political dissent. As the 'Prada Meinhof' principle suggests, the passage of time can lend even the most ardent of terms a somewhat *recherche* quality. Guy Debord liked to call this commodification of ideas into items of leisure *récupération*. More than any other political writer or work, Debord and his publication *The Society of the Spectacle* (1967) are often referenced as the theoretical link between the two dates. His critique of capitalist society was underpinned by a vision of society blinded by the shining promotion of unreal ideals.

Westwood & McLaren, Tom of Finland 'Cowboy' T-shirt, 1975.

The continuing appeal of these dates and the youth-based clothes that offered themselves as their sartorial signifiers is due to the weight of authenticity that the sociological study of subcultural dress has borne down upon them. The wearing of this kind of counter-cultural dress very much trades upon its sociological definition, long defined by the work of Dick Hebdige. More than any other street, the King's Road is most closely connected to the idea of wearing particular clothes in a particular way and walking down a particular street as subcultural practice. From the infamous journey that Alan Jones made from Seditionaries in August 1975 along the King's Road wearing his new purchase of the Tom of Finland T-shirt, before being arrested on Piccadilly for indecent exposure, to the Straight-Up portraits of punks that appeared in the first issues of i-D magazine, the primacy of subcultural dress is located in how it is played out on the street.

Much of this kind of sociological analysis tends to regard the interiors of retail spaces and their façades as mere sites of consumption, rather than for their ability to harness cultural ideas in visual form. This is very much in evidence in Hebdige's crucial text *Subculture: The Meaning of Style* (1979), which begins by discussing a passage from *The Thief's Journal* by Jean Genet, a writer he saw as closest to his object of study, and one he used as a model for the construction of style in subculture.

The opening quote that Hebdige uses describes the walls of Genet's prison cell, decorated with faces of criminals torn from newspapers pasted to the wall with chewed bits of bread. He then discusses how a tube of Vaseline confiscated from the prison cell becomes a symbol of Genet's triumph over the repressive order of the prison and is thus emblematic of a mundane object that is transformed through style into a symbol of refusal. This is then applied as a motif for Hebdige's own analysis of how clothing is similarly transformed in subcultural dress.

What is surprising is that Hebdige totally ignores the significance of Genet's decorated cell. His oversight is very typical of how youth subcultural identity and dress has often been studied – either isolated or in the context of the street, but never in relation to the decorated retail interior that stimulates the practice. If you consider Genet's shrine in relation to a description of the Let It Rock shop by Craig Bromberg, the parallel between the two interiors is only too easy to appreciate. What they demonstrate is the centrality of the shop interior to an understanding of a style position and how it is able to frame its many references:

> The Year is 1972, but inside it's supposed to be 1956 ... These Teddy Boys here – just as much an anachronism as that old radio with the twist-knob or the reddish angle poise lamp with the fifties

Price-list for 'Let It Rock', King's Road, Chelsea.

shade near the till – want to know if there's any beer in the garish
pink n' black fridge at the back of the shop. No one listens to them
. . . Everyone nods in dim tribute to the photographs of James
Dean and Brigitte Bardot glaring at the world from their frames of
glued-up looking-glass shards. Next to the pinned-up fake leopard

skin, the advert for Vince's Man Shop of Carnaby Street ... the torn photographs from Men Only and Light & Sound, the display case with the fifties rayon ties, the metal studs and the neon green striped socks, one of the Teds is looking over a barren rack of lovingly copied drape jackets.[2]

This is also a space of homage, highly reminiscent of prison-cell wall decoration in its tear-and-paste technique, but this is a shrine to the vitality of the Teddy Boys and rock 'n' roll – youth culture's first fit of resistance. Let It Rock was Malcolm McLaren's and Vivienne Westwood's first shop to affront the hippy sensibilities of shoppers on the King's Road through a rearguard embrace of an earlier and more violent expression of youth culture. It was constructed to create as much an air of menace and criminality as Genet's cell, from its glass-shard frames of heroes to its homoerotic imagery torn from old sales catalogues from Vince's: disruption was crucial.

The problem that subcultural analysis has with retail spaces lies in their ability to change 'secret' objects into commodities fit for public consumption. This transformation from objects that aid resistance to objects that speed diffusion is a challenge to their understanding that subcultural dress is fashioned from the street rather than selected from a pre-digested array of consumables. Even more of an anathema to someone like Hebdige is the notion of revival or pastiche; he termed the Ted revival of the 1970s in which Let It Rock played a central part in as 'situated somewhere between the Fonz of television's Happy Days and a recycled Ovaltine ad'.[3] By claiming that revivals are redolent of passivity (indulging in bedtime drinks and watching programmes about the good old days), Hebdige sees them as opposite to the vitality of authentic sub-cultural practice; but the two products of popular culture referred to are very much symptomatic of an interest in retrochic that came to the fore at the end of the 1960s and that also ran through the 1970s. As a princi-ple of stylistic evolution based upon the plundering of past styles, it pro-duced a strange and hybrid aesthetic that drew upon many references.

The close relationship that many stylistic entrepreneurs of boutique culture had not only with fashion but also with the antique and auction markets made them adept at sourcing both clothing and decorative arts, and this was to have a strong impact on how they furnished their retail spaces and the clothing styles they adopted to sell. These kinds of relationships between clothing and decorative arts can be understood within a broader phenomenon where decorative trends are informed by exhibitions reappraising the work of the past, the resurrection of particular artists, the preservation of architecture, the appropriation of stylistic forms and the dissemination of filmic style.

Retrochic, as it became known, began in the 1970s at the Marché aux Puces in Paris by people interested in how the decorative styles of the 1930s revived the links between fashion and cinema (eventually coining the neologism Art Deco). A particularly pertinent designer is Karl Lagerfeld. His work for Chloe between 1969 and 1972 developed the revival of Art Nouveau and Art Deco in a manner that mirrored the amassing of his own private Art Deco furniture collection. What began as a minority taste, an eccentricity, quickly developed into an alternative model of consumerism backed by a strong enterprise culture.

In London, retrochic appeared through the trading of similar kinds of decorative arts and fashions, but it also traced a connection to a prior impulse to look to the past for pleasure. In his study of retromania and our nation's love of the past Raphael Samuel claimed that:

> In its play aspect, its love of dressing up, and its taste for histrionics retrochic rejoins, and could be seen as a late offspring of, that self-indulgent strain in British national taste which design historians see as a kind of antiphon to the austerities of post-war Britain.[4]

Samuel, of course, is referring to the Festival of Britain staged in London in 1951, but instead of the modernity of the Pylon and textile designs based on molecular structures, he identifies retrochic with the Battersea Pleasure Gardens and *The Unsophisticated Arts* exhibition at the Whitechapel Art Gallery, which celebrated the naive and popular arts and crafts as another and equal-aspect influence on post-war Britain.

The work of the pop artist Peter Blake, for example, combined the
allure of contemporary American popular culture with the whimsical
relics found in London's antique markets. It too underlines that retrochic
can be understood as an interest in the picturesque, which is as powerful
in its evocation of imagination, wit and delight as the pop-like pull of
modernity found in all things new. It suggests a status for retrochic not so
much defined as inferior to the signal strength of pop, but equal to pop
and invested with an emotional value that makes it distinct.

Fairground murals, vernacular imagery and hand-crafted Victorian
letter forms were used by the artist Michael English in his hand-painted
mural designs for the shop front of Nigel Weymouth's Granny Takes a
Trip on the King's Road and Michael Rainey's Hung on You at 430 King's
Road, occupying the retail site prior to Paradise Garage. The work of
Michael English is useful in demonstrating how retrochic hardened as it
moved across the eight-year span. His mural designs for the aforemen-
tioned shop fronts had all the crispness and clarity of Pop Art paintings
and served as graphical calling cards that were more legible than street
signs. His subsequent development of an English form of psychedelic
poster art, published under the company name Hapsash and the
Coloured Coat, produced an illustrational style that matched a drug-
induced state to a heady concoction of decorative and historical referents. George Melly likened it to a 'a rubbery synthesis of Early Disney
and Mabel Lucy Atwell carried to the edge of illegibility . . . almost a collage of other men's hard won visions: Mucha, Ernst, Magritte, Bosch,
William Blake, comic books, engravings of Red Indians, Disney, Dulac,
ancient illustrations of treatises on alchemy: everything is boiled down
to make a visionary and hallucinatory bouillabaisse'.[5]

The warped designs became emblematic of the visual surfacing of
the underground culture that London spawned in the late 1960s, but at
the same time it referred back to the decadent culture of the 1890s,
recently revisited in the hugely popular exhibition of Aubrey Beardsley
at the Victoria and Albert Museum in 1966. As Melly was right to assert,
English's posters were powerful concoctions that graphically mapped
the historical connections that modernity had tried to erase.

Yet by 1970 English had abandoned the psychedelic style and had

The shop front of the 'Hung On You' boutique in Cale Street, Chelsea, 10 February 1967.

The 'Granny Takes a Trip' mural being painted.

Michael English, 'Coke' from *The Rubbish Prints*, 1970, airbrush.

instead moved into environmental happenings, oil-lamp projections and the medium of airbrush. His airbrush designs based on the theme of rubbish, particularly his close-up view of a discarded Coke bottle top, were to become the most popular posters of the period, sold in their millions by Athena. His Hyper-Realist style was celebrated for its level of detail and its ability to make the most mundane things look extraordinary, but they harness an aesthetic that connects the late 1960s with the late 1970s.

Here the detritus of modern life, most specifically an American-inspired one, became the focus for an aesthetic that celebrated a hollowness that glorified surface over any desire for substance or idealism. It was a figuring of the 'flowers in the dustbin' as a desirable state before punk had appropriated it. Philip Castle is the other airbrush artist who made this connection. As a student at the Royal College of Art in the late 1960s, he commandeered an old airbrush that students had been using to re-spray their scooters in the prevailing spirit of mural design. He took the tool and taught himself how to replicate on paper the chrome and tailfins of American car culture, before putting these skills to the test for commercial fashion advertising, most notably for Pretty Polly tights. It was these ads that gave Castle the commission to produce the poster for Stanley Kubrick's *A Clockwork Orange* (1971) – a relevant example of super-smooth rendering, sugar-coated images of unbridled violence.

The metamorphosis of the Granny Takes a Trip façade documents a similar hardening of image: from the totemic face of the Red Indian, to the front half of an actual American Dodge car set in front of a display of psychedelic posters, to the shop front covered in graffiti and the Dodge vandalized. The shop front traces a move from a fairly simplistic appropriation of historical imagery, through hallucinatory visions and the reflective and hollow surfaces of American popular culture to a vision of neglect and decay. In its mutation it charts the empty airbrush aesthetic of the 1970s as having grown from the burgeoning mural design of the late 1960s.

Another stylistic entrepreneur whose career mapped these changes is Tommy Roberts, who came from a tradition of entrepreneurship that made him the first British person to open an Italian-style coffee bar in the 1950s, and then turn his hand to selling a hippy-chic array of bells and beads at Kleptomania on Carnaby Street in the late 60s. Hailing from south-east London from the home of a bookmaker and music-hall artist (as a journalist once noted, he looks like a bit of both), Roberts attended Goldsmiths College for a year, before McLaren, and then went into the antiques trade.

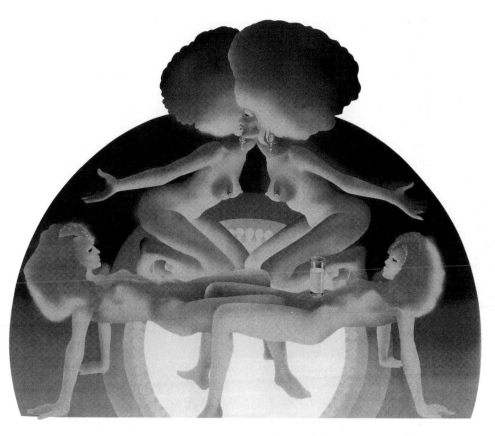

Philip Castle, 'Korova Milk Bar Scene', design for *A Clockwork Orange*, 1971

The opening of Mr Freedom at 430 King's Road in 1969 (two years before Let It Rock) was a meeting of fashion and Pop Art that was an instant success with the style press. Roberts's colours of bright reds, acid blues, gaudy satins, pop symbols of comic-strip space rockets and cartoon characters, slogans such as 'pow!' and 'slip it to me' all enjoyed influential status, most famously for being appropriated for Yves Saint Laurent's ready-to-wear collection for 1970.

The interior of the shop featured a central mirror ball that illuminated turquoise-blue walls, ceiling and carpet and included an 8-foot-

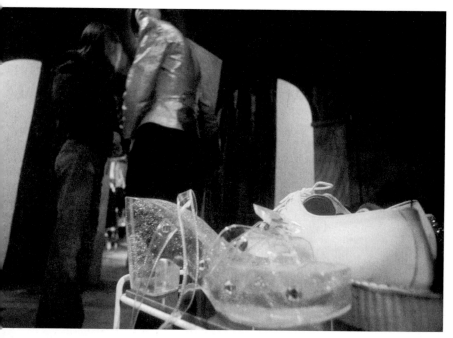

Mr Freedom, Kensington Church Street, 1970s.

high blue stuffed gorilla and a counter with televisions set into its frame. However, the fun furniture Roberts sold was important in crystallizing ideas from Italian design and American architectural theory in a fashion context. A mixture of Claus Oldenburg's soft sculptures, the surrealism of Salvador Dalí's Mae West Lips sofa and a childlike sense of fun created forms such as a false-teeth chair, a sofa formed from a pile of oversized cigarettes, giant match lamp standards and Liquorice Allsorts cushions. These artefacts were conscious not only of their design references, but also of their dissemination, surreally fulfilling the design historian Reyner Banham's observation on colour supplement culture that 'previously unselfconscious and virtually invisible domestic items suddenly become great, monumental objects which demand attention, dusting and illustration in colour supplements'.[6]

Many of Roberts's commercial ideas were in keeping with the debates initiated by the design community about the nature of the postmodern. In 1968 Corin Hughes-Stanton wrote an article in *Design* magazine that defined a new use of the term postmodern, which had previously been used by the architectural critic Nikolaus Pevsner to describe the late buildings of Le Corbusier. Hughes-Stanton used it to describe a new form of design that was either in disregard or ignorance of modernist principles, and the example he chose to illustrate this were the Union-Jack-emblazoned goods of Carnaby Street (he probably even saw Roberts selling them):

> As an attitude [Post-modernism] is closer to people and to what they want: it is prepared to meet all their legitimate needs without moralising about what those needs should be. Its roots are thus deeper imbedded in society than those of the modern school.[7]

The article proposed that the combination of fashionable expendability, a responsive catering to popular taste and an understanding of the symbolism of decorative form should be construed as postmodern. In looking at the clothing and furniture designs of Mr Freedom, one can certainly agree that they bear the hallmarks of this combination: as pleasurable eye candy that instantly gratify. But the way in which these goods were consumed was not in the knowledge of them being thought of as postmodern, but for how they challenged notions of acceptable taste.

A prominent facet of postmodernism is how it offered alternative histories that could represent minority cultures; much of this was informed by the material culture trawled through the practice of retrochic that offered and afforded the trappings of alternative strategies. For the feminist writer Kaja Silvermann, vintage clothes became the only feasible means for a feminist visibly to reject the prevailing discourse of femininity without abandoning a love of fashion. For other minority groups seeking emancipation, retrochic offered a myriad of propositions. Philip Core wonderfully sums up the liberation this permitted in the 1970s through an objectified kind of permissiveness in his book *Camp: The Lie that Tells the Truth*:

1950s memorabilia, first collected by Duggie Fields in London, has flooded advertising and generated a whole range of imitations through shops like Christopher Strangeways. Straight undergraduates wore make-up in the seventies. The suburbs collect Clarice Cliff porcelain and mirrored coffee tables. Drag queens meet royalty. Beaton photographs reach record prices in the salerooms.[8]

Here camp is articulated and disseminated not through obvious sites of performance, but through recycled material culture, sifted and graded before being bestowed on stratified markets. The flaunting of 'Bad' taste so as to appear better than good was a crucial feature of this trend; as an article from *Vogue* in 1971 featuring Mr Freedom and Biba asked: 'Is bad taste such a bad thing?'[9]

This consciousness is very much supported by the copy printed in the *Biba Newspaper*, given to customers at the opening of Biba's ultimate shop on the site of the former Derry & Toms department store in

Biba at Derry & Toms, Kensington High Street, 1975.

Kensington. It read: 'A small museum devoted to Grave Lapses From
Good Taste. Everything in Biba's kitsch department is guaranteed to
be as camp as Aldershot. Nothing here will ever make the Design
Centre, but shrewd investors could buy now with an eye on Sotheby's
in 1993.'

The prophecy was strangely fulfilled; Phillips Auctioneers in
London did have an auction in 1993 that featured Biba furniture. But
bad, good or otherwise, this new take on fashionable style was not to
everyone's taste. In 1971 the Situationist-inspired British guerrilla
group King Mob attempted to bomb Biba, stating in their distributed
pamphlets: 'in fashion as in everything else, capitalism can only go
backwards'. As temples of consumption, department stores had long
been an object of fascination for the Situationist International. The
methods of spectacle and display were the perfect accessories for the
demonstration of Debord's principles of spectacle, but they were also
the ideal means through which one could promote these subversive
ideas.

In 1969 while at Goldsmiths, Malcolm McLaren made a film concerning Oxford Street that was intended to support Debord's theories and to
act as a catalyst to awake consumers against consumption. The film
aimed to articulate the hollowness of capitalism, the apathy and frustra-
tion of consumers and the modelling of Oxford Street as a retail space
that offered 'no relaxation, geared totally to work and consumption'.

Featuring footage from Selfridges, the only department store to
allow them access for filming, and Mr Freedom on the King's Road, the
film was inspired by the Gordon Riots of the eighteenth century and
was intended to induce a violent uprising. It included a section that
considered fan worship as a facet of spectacle, and it included an interview with the head of the Billy Fury fan club. This section of the film
was labelled 'the glitter of the signs' and was to prove itself as the
research necessary to set McLaren and Westwood up as retailers of Ted
clothing.

By investing in a form of youth culture that was now long in the
tooth, McLaren and Westwood began to sell items that chimed with
Guy Debord's view of fad objects, which turned absurdity into 'a com-

A Mr Freedom man's T-shirt, cotton with satin appliqué, 1970–71.

modity in its own right'. They realized that this absurdity could be sold and worn as a perverse form of resistance to the dominating themes of consumerism. Let It Rock was their first experiment, and many were to follow, but always with the combination of a provocative title, absurd commodities and a deliberate interior scheme. Many claim that the resistance that they created was a pleasure of the perverse that was played out in the wearing of their clothes. But once again, this view denies the importance of the retail shop interior and exterior in staging these subversions.

The appreciation of spectacle shared by all the retailers and practitioners I have examined is rarely praised or even identified. An article on London retail design by Dejan Sudjic for *Architectural Review* remains a small exception:

> Three questionable design trends have emerged in London recently. The most harmless is a form of anti-shop that deters all but the most resolute from entering. The second is one more growth of American sub-culture tastelessness in the form of a hamburger chain. The designs are not so much vulgar as eclectically null. Finally, the latest example of the cult of preservation: the incorporation in a cinema of a kiosk and bar designed in variations of ephemeral *moderne* style which gave stylistic zip to the tasteless 20s.[10]

The article reviewed a fashion boutique on the King's Road called Plaza owned by Antony Price, a McDonald's restaurant and a refurbished Odeon cinema in the area, each representing a particular strain of influence on retail design in London the late 1970s.

The 'anti-shop that deters all but the most resolute from entering' is not just Plaza, but is representative of the kind of boutique retail design in question. It was a shop façade that acted neither as window display nor advertiser of goods, but as a defiant advertisement – not necessarily an invitation to enter, but a statement to enter at risk. Therefore, the façade assumes what Debord considered 'not a negation of style, but a style of negation'.[11]

The industrial yet hand-crafted designs that many of these retailers developed for their shop fascias maintained a visible tension between the charge of the street and the charge of the wares on sale inside. They invited the possibility of a mismatch between the reality of the every-day by buying into the unreality of the goods of yesterday's tomorrow. From English's mural for Hung On You, Jon Wealleans's work for Mr Freedom, the Electric Colour Company's façade for Paradise Garage, Westwood's and McLaren's assemblages for Let It Rock and Sex, lead-ing to David Conner's and Ben Kelly's famously fearful shopfront for Seditionaries in late 1976, all were responses to the notion of the mass-produced spectacle. But in producing a hand-crafted quotation that acted as a fascia, they questioned whether 'spectacle' really was all about manufacture and oppression.

When making her film about the rise of punk, Janet Street-Porter asked Trevor Miles what the King's Road was like at the end of a Saturday afternoon and he replied:

> Well the sort of debris, It's like Brighton. Its like spending a day at Brighton with all the tourists and all the people and the rocks and everything . . . It's very similar to that you know, the debris and the cleaning up the mess. It's great fun though.[12]

Miles encapsulates the view of fashion retailing not merely as spec-tacle, but also as a form of performed entertainment. In likening the King's Road to Brighton beach we can appreciate how a shopping dis-trict operates in a manner not dissimilar to a seaside promenade in terms of the pleasure and leisure it affords. But Miles's response is not all sunshine – it insinuates that not everyone is on their day off; and that there are those who labour to service the experience on a daily basis. A crucial surviving example of Mr Freedom's t-shirt designs at Manchester Art Gallery is emblazoned with a graphical image of an ice-cream wafer. As an item of fashion sold on the King's Road it very much supports Miles's analogy to Brighton.

Yet if we consider it against Grail Marcus's view that Pinkie and his gang, the protagonists of Graham Greene's novel *Brighton Rock* (1938), are the literary precursors to the punks of the King's Road, we can also appreciate the seedy underside to this vision: the sense of dissatisfaction and illegal opportunity in lives lived to support the workings of a pleasure resort. It underlines how one of the most important cultural expressions of the late twentieth century is formed from this climate of entertainment, from a boutique culture proficient in dressing the retailing of fashion in ideas that resisted the very nature of consumerism.

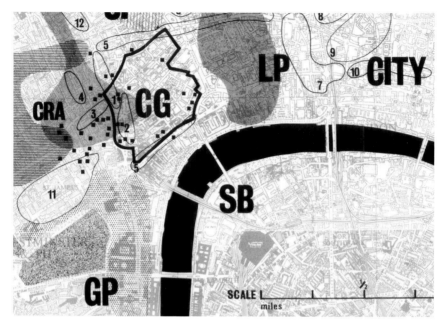

Map from 'Covent Garden's Moving: Covent Garden Area Draft Plan' published by the Consortium of Greater London Council, City of Westminster, London Borough of Camden.

CHAPTER SEVEN

*Remaining on the King's Road, this chapter starts with an out-
right rejection of youth and subculture – a trip to the department
store Peter Jones. It was here that the fashion designer Scott Crolla
had the idea of buying chintz furnishing fabric and making a suit
out of it for a fancy-dress party. As an idea it was the starting
point for the resurgence of interest in floral forms in the 1980s,
on a scale not seen since the 1960s.*

*In the mid-1980s areas of London began to bloom – not with
actual flowers, but with representations of them. Unlike the
flower power of the 1960s, which symbolized peace, love and
pacifist principles, this was a different kind of flower power that
traded upon the potent historical connotations that certain flower
forms visually convey.*

The blossoming of heavy rose heads in deep reds and pinks on a pale ground, commonly known as chintz, started emerging in London on all manner of consumables – not just curtains and cushions, but on record covers, in magazine articles and on men's shirts. This kind of visual quotation is very much emblematic of how the past was integrated into the present in the 1980s, as a kind of symbolism with a thin surface depth, and a kind worn lightly.

The area of Covent Garden in London and its redevelopment into a shopping area in the 1980s mirrors this shift: from the selling of real flowers, to representations of flowers printed on fashionable goods for sale. As early as 1968 urban planners had considered the redevelopment of Covent Garden in advance of the Fruit and Flower Markets moving in 1974 to a new and larger location in Vauxhall, south London. Yet the economic stagnation of the 1970s and a change in attitude towards architectural conservation left the area barren and boarded-up for a number of years. It eventually afforded the salvaging of Market House, designed by Charles Fowler, into the centrepiece for a new form of small-scale retailing for a shopping district that traded as much on the boutique culture of the post-war period as it did on the market trading of nineteenth-century London. This overlay of two different kinds of historic retailing gave the buying of fashionable goods in Covent Garden a particular charge: it was about buying into something new, but also something old at one and the same time. It may sound no different from the retrochic of the 1970s, but this was newer: it was retrochic with value-added heritage.

This fusing of the old and the new runs through many of the flower-patterned examples with which this chapter deals, showing how the consumption of floral forms was an attempt to reconnect with historical ideals about being able to view London as a garden village rather than a city. Much of the need to reclaim the neglected areas of central London, such as Soho, by the young creative professionals of the 1980s was bound by the desire to make pockets of central London appear smaller and more manageable to live in; or, it was to make areas appear like a forgotten pleasure garden from its past. Indeed, after the fruit and flower market moved out, Covent Garden became a fertile playground for those young and creative 'flowers in the dustbin' who were interested in abandoning the vestiges of punk and slipping into something a little more playful. The opening of the Blitz nightclub in 1979, at a small wine bar next door to the Masonic Temple in Covent Garden, was the setting for the birth of the New Romantics, the art-school heroes who raided the dressing-up box of the past on a nightly basis. The clothes they wore were often bought from what they found in the area, be it vintage shirting and military overcoats from the shop PX run by Roger Burton, or furs and capes from the closing-down sale of the theatrical costumiers Charles Fox in Covent Garden.

The style commentator Peter York described the club as 'the first great fancy dress party of the eighties',[1] and this notion of costume and masquerade remained important to many of these floral expressions and to fashion design sensibilities found in London in the 1980s. All reflected a mischievous and creative hybrid of historical references in a bid to look different, even if it were only for an evening.

In a small showcase article for emerging menswear designers in London printed in *Harpers & Queen* in February 1985, Scott Crolla (wearing one of his own suits) described the design references he drew upon for his outfit. In stating 'azaleas, The Doors, The Duke of Wellington's suits, St Ives, orange and purple, the Brompton Oratory, Gilbert & George, delphiniums, double cuffs in Croydon, hairy shirts in Whitehall and a hatred of modern classics' one can appreciate how the suit he was wearing, although fairly simple in form, was heavily laden with meaning.

Not unlike all the other art-school heroes, Crolla was a progressive fine art graduate who found simple referencing unpoetic. His intoxicatingly fragrant list evokes heady combinations: heavy blossomed flowers straining to the musical apotheosis of 'flower power' in psychedelic flames; the perfunctory detailing of the modern male business suit in Croydon unhinged by the posturing of Gilbert and George in Spitalfields; the soot-stained visions of rank, church and politics in London colour-saturated by the light of St Ives. These vividly clashing combinations were intended to underline their combined difference to modern classics, such as those products promoted by design writers such as Deyan Sudjic, editor of the magazine *Blueprint*, whose publication

Scott Crolla, spring/summer 1985 collection, London.

'Cult Objects' praised Filofaxes and Braun toasters, or the 1980s vision of the 'matt-black dream-home' that was strictly limited edition.

Unlike the rational references of these modernist objects, the products of fashion are resolutely drawn from illogical and unorthodox sources. The suitability of fashion as a historical model for defining what a postmodern sensibility could be, particularly in its magpie method of sourcing and representing history, made claims such as Crolla's important material in design debates of the time. Indeed, in 1988 Caroline Evans and Minna Thornton wrote that the fashion caption (just like the one made by Crolla) in the British style magazine of the 1980s was a central example of postmodern sensibility, in its ability to render pastiche and marginality.[2]

The *Harpers & Queen* menswear article was titled 'Fad Togs for Englishmen', punning Noël Coward's Las Vegas stage favourite *Mad Dogs and Englishmen*. It suggests a textual play upon lyrical sentiments, where the idea of what an Englishmen should wear is laced with a self-deprecating humour and a somewhat historicized view of correct form. Although proclaiming the peculiarity of Englishmen taking the midday sun, Coward never personally vouched for the pastime, presenting himself as somehow beyond it by the very Englishness of his own dress and demeanour, as an extreme form of pastiche. It follows, then, that a designer such as Crolla had much to learn from the affectation of the milieu of Coward as performer and raconteur in Las Vegas – as much, perhaps, as the postmodern architect Robert Venturi had learnt from the city's surface architecture in his seminal architectural text 'Learning from Las Vegas'.[3]

One of Crolla's most influential contributions to clothing for men and women in the period – which was aped by all levels of the clothing market – was the use of chintz cotton as a shirting and suiting fabric,

Scott Crolla, spring/summer 1985 collection, London, featuring Sir Hugh Casson.

Scott Crolla, spring/summer 1985 collection, London.

devised in conjunction with his partner Georgina Godley. It was as odd
a combination as Coward in Las Vegas, but it communicated a vision of
Englishness just as brashly. In transposing a surface design used primarily for domestic interior decoration into a pattern for sartorial display,
Crolla and Godley indicated an affinity between a certain form of architectural design and a certain form of dress. What was explicit about this
use of chintz was the idea that you were wearing history, but a sense of
history informed by the historicism of period decoration. Further, it
was not about presenting history as something lifeless, but as something that you performed when you wore it.

This aspect very much chimes with the first use of the furnishing
fabric by Crolla for a fancy-dress outfit he designed for himself. As he
recounts:

> I was invited to a 'Piers Gaveston' party at the Dorchester or
> some other hotel and the theme was The Garden of Earthly
> Delights. I went to Peter Jones, bought some curtain fabric and
> made a Nehru suit. *Women's Wear Daily* took a photo – people

seemed to like it, so I put the suit in the store. Chris Difford of
Squeeze bought it and then I made more.[4]

As the presence of the *Women's Wear Daily* photographer proves, Crolla's chintz creations appeared at the same moment that London once again began to be courted by international buyers, who had started to kindle interest in London Fashion Week as a fixture on the international fashion calendar worth attending. Not since the 1960s had London gained such interest for the scope of its creativity, supported by an established art school system that was producing a range of motivated designers inspired by their integration with London club culture and their reflections in an eager style press. In this short-lived instance, the status of London as a fashion capital was informed by designers who were inspired by the metaphorical role the city could play in their designs. A seasonal bloom of floral fabrics was therefore not merely a trend but a mythical representation of Englishness defined in its coded specificity to spaces and places held in the historical fabric of London and, in turn, elsewhere.

The idea of a man wearing an outfit covered in rose blooms to a party was not particularly new. It is likely that Crolla was aware of the famous Cecil Beaton fancy-dress jacket of 1937, now owned by the Victoria and Albert Museum. Beaton designed the jacket himself and wore it to a *Fête champêtre* he gave with Michael Duff at his country house at Ashcombe in the summer of 1937. The party itself was a very British response to the ideas of Surrealism, transforming unsettling imagery into light and decorative touches: servants wore animal and bird masks inspired by ones that Beaton had seen with Salvador Dalí in Venice. Beaton's jacket was cut in a mock eighteenth-century style in cream corduroy; it was appliquéd with large pink roses made from netting and muslin and was dotted with cracked eggshells and egg whites made from imitation plastic.

The outfit reflects the interesting intersection between the use of natural forms such as florals and foliage in fashion printed textiles and the Surrealists' use of them as disturbing visual tropes that were used as stand-ins for the human form. Beaton made this his own, as did many other British Surrealists, by codifying it within the English landscape. So, his jacket was the English rose garden supplanted, the farmyard hatched. The beauty of it was that it traded as much on the vogue for Surrealism as it did on the visions stoked in Lewis Carroll's nineteenth-century children's story *Alice Through the Looking-Glass*. The potions that Alice swallows in the tale, which turn her very big or very small, are dream-like plays with scale that are rather symbolic of the way that floral furnishing fabrics were used by Crolla and others in the 1980s.

Crolla's trip to Peter Jones on the King's Road is significant, since the fabric he bought, produced by Sandersons, was a chintz named after the area he bought it in. Sanderson produced three scaled versions of the design in a number of colour ways: the smallest in scale titled 'Minor Chelsea', then 'Little Chelsea' and then the largest, simply called 'Chelsea'. As a family of designs they indicate not only the scale of the design but also map an understanding of the area of Chelsea, past and present. As such, it is easy to see them as an equivalent to the fashion caption of the British style magazine, as another striking motif of post-modern design practice.

Little Chelsea
Furnishing Fabric,
Sandersons.

Wallace Stevens once made the observation that 'people do not live in places but in the description of places'. It therefore follows that 'Little Chelsea' is not merely a geographical place name, but also a term in the language of floral design. In Crolla's hands, it also maps the language of fashion to specific networks in time and space.

Little Chelsea was the name given to a hamlet in the mid-eighteenth century that ran from the World's End to the boundary of Fulham, set in the space between Cremorne Gardens and Brompton Cemetery. The first wave of building had brought sizeable house estates to the land, but by the nineteenth century it had developed into a village of small cobbled multi-occupied streets of dense building, gaining it a picturesque quality that appealed to many for its supposed neighbourliness. Its attraction was that it lay beyond the poor air of London and yet was near enough for travel to and from the City, but its status as 'the scented village' was due to the number of horticultural businesses in the area, the first being the Royal Exotic Nursery, which opened in the mid-eighteenth century. These nurseries contributed not only to the historical cultivation of the English garden, but also to the adaptation of tropical plants to the English climate. The desirability of the area was such that in 1748 a young man advertising for a wife offered a home in Chelsea 'midst the floral beauties of the King's Road'.[5] This history is directly linked to the Chelsea Flower Show that still runs today.

In *English Culture and the Decline of the Industrial Spirit* (1981), Martin J. Wiener claims that two contrasting symbols were used in the nineteenth century to express England: the Garden, what we might recognize as our 'Green and Pleasant Land', and the Workshop, referring to our industrialized nation. The symbols are also useful for their application to an understanding of the City. So, if Little Chelsea is the Garden, then the City of London is the Workshop. London as a Garden is thus a place where one hopes to avoid the stresses of urban life by inhaling the scent of tamed nature. Here, the evocation of Little Chelsea is for a way of metropolitan living lost, one that was once on the periphery, but now marks the ring of the city's urbanized core. The oppositional elements of the rural and the urban are forged in a construct without geographical referents, but that network an English sensibility: the stillness of domesticity, craft and the garden fixed in bloom.

Writing in the *Chelsea Society Annual Report* in 1980, Charlotte Gore lamentably catalogued the erosion of a traditional high street in Chelsea to fashion retail, but presciently captured the misapprehension that was rapidly modifying the area:

> Chelsea is widely but I think mistakenly regarded as being a despoilt village – a little larger than life . . . but full of the traces of modest elegance and abundant greenery that poignantly recall an idyllic past.[6]

The property market of the 1980s stretched the boundaries of Chelsea beyond credibility and peddled the projection of a genteel garden with cottage-scale housing. The neighbouring town of Battersea, south of the Thames, a working-class backwater since the 1950s, was also reclaimed for its proximity to Chelsea; it was transformed, in similar terms, through the constant reiteration of the word 'village' for its central square, and its re-naming by estate agents as South Chelsea. This reclaiming of the Victorian suburbs by the young middle classes in the 1980s was also a generational move, for those whose parents had initially vacated to the New Towns of the post-war period for a better life. As such, this form of property investment reflected not only a wish to repossess the metropolis, but also a desire to reject the suburban modernism bestowed upon a previous generation.

The return migration by young professionals to dwellings once inhabited by their forefathers was not only a rediscovery of Victorian architectural space, but also a rediscovery of an older, bourgeois repudiation of modernism. Chintz bears strong associations to its use in the 1920s and '30s as a fabric for domestic decoration, so those who wore it in the 1980s were claiming in visual terms an ironic link between their own ideas about the past and the past of their grandparents.

Many of those who returned to Victorian housing stock found that the revealing of period features involved ripping off the hardboard from panelled doors and boxed-in fireplaces: the effects of the previous generation's piecemeal efforts to make their homes look as seamless as possible, in keeping with modernist trends for the interior. The product designer Danny Weil, who had become well known in design circles for a radio that held the technological components in a transparent plastic pouch rather than a conventional casing, produced another radio design in 1985 that played with the historical connotations of chintz and the post-war renovation of the domestic interior.

The three-band radio design was titled Small Door; it was produced in a limited edition of twenty and was exhibited in 1985 at the Architectural Association in London. This goes a long way in demonstrating the status of British product design at this time. The radio looked as if a plywood louvre door, propped by trestle legs, was being

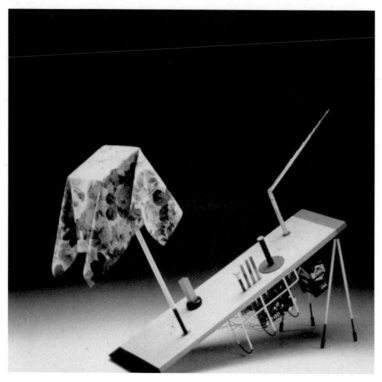

Daniel Weil, *Small Door* three-band radio, 1985.

used as a tabletop with a bray of valves rising from its surface and a piece of floral chintz floating above. On closer inspection, the door became reminiscent of a piece of wood from a Roberts radio, that most traditional of English radios; further, the chintz fabric seemed as if it were a cover for a budgerigar cage, thrown over at night to prevent the bird from singing. Weil used these two sounds of domesticity in the post-war English interior as the visual means to represent the purpose of the radio. The design became a celebrated example of how the forms of the past could be utilized as the interface through which a user could engage with the purpose of a product.

This example claims chintz as a kitsch facet of the interior decoration tastes of the 1920s and '30s, but it would be wrong to claim the historical charge of chintz as being this simplistic, because this historical connection merely carries us to a broader and more complicated set of values around national identity, one established by the Victorians but upheld well into the twentieth century. The formulation of a mythical and timeless sense of Englishness by Victorian intellectuals rested very much on the distinction between the Garden and the Workshop, its stillness in opposition to the rhythm of industry and the mark of the hand so characteristic of artisanal production was often its visual indicator, as were floral forms.

The popularity of fabrics such as chintz in establishing this position was not only on account of the flora that evoked the traditionalists' view of England as garden, but also for chintz's colonial history as a printed fabric inscribed and modified by the commercial trade between India and Britain. As a fabric it can be traced back to the origins of trading between Asia and Europe in the 1600s, and its popularity amongst the French and English as an Indian fabric to be worn. By 1700 the crown demanded that the wearing of chintz made from imported Indian fabric should be banned in order to facilitate the growth of a British textile industry, which could rival the colour, complexity and detail of such quality fabrics. (At the time, more than six million pieces of chintz were arriving annually from Bengal.) Chintz, then, can be understood as a pictorial image that presents imperialism as a civilizing and taming force; it presents nature as domesticated for the interior in the same way that the village is seen to tame nature within the city.

Chintz was very much emblematic of the 'splendid isolation' of England as Garden, structured by the broader territories of Empire. In its use in clothing design in the 1980s, it can also be claimed as emblematic of postmodern subjectivity. Fredric Jameson defined this new kind of subjectivity as a form of cognitive mapping where individual experience is not informed solely by the locale, but by broader coordinates, and he used the example of the everyday experience of London as being networked across the older, colonial system of Empire.

An emblem such as chintz, then, became the visual means by which these broader coordinates could be momentarily mapped. What this suggests is that the consumption of chintz in London in the 1980s networked historical and geographical referents that could be claimed as signifying postmodern urban experience. Yet many have argued that what might have constituted this experience and the urban regeneration that postmodernism brought about in the 1980s was just a recycled vision of nineteenth-century Romanticism that celebrated nostalgia and mourned loss. A postmodern use of chintz, however, can be seen just as much as a reworking of the nineteenth-century delight in imagination, fancy and the treasuring of keepsakes.

The interest in chintz as a furnishing fabric for the interior may well have been fuelled by this sentiment, but it was not merely a case of ransacking the past for suitable fragments, since it was in fact far more studious. The demand for authentic reproductions in the furnishing market and the improvement in screen-printing technologies meant that by the 1980s a commercial imperative found uses for eighteenth- and nineteenth-century pattern books that had all but been forgotten. Their timely 'rediscovery' was to bring museological rigour to the dating of designs and the correctness of their decorative application. One of the biggest 'recoveries' was the Courtauld collection of more than 3,000 designs, including one named 'Chelsea Bouquet'. The attraction of chintz in interior decoration terms was the way in which it could project into a space a haunting vision of the past: of an abandoned rose garden in full bloom.

This idea of haunting a space with blooms was also enacted by the short-lived fashion designers Mark & Syrie, who were big on ideas but short on finance. Faced at the last minute with being unable to stage their first show in the venue they wanted because of lack of money, they managed to persuade the chaplain of St George's Church off Hanover Square to let them stage their collection in the churchyard. They then walked the press around from the original venue to the church and presented clothes dripping in rose blooms woven into a rug material worn on a hot summer's day. St George's was, in its Regency heyday, the most fashionable church in which to get married, so the show was an accidental, but poetic tribute to all those who had also walked the yard carrying a bouquet. For their next collection, Mark & Syrie made outfits from branded beer towels bought from pubs (see p. 11), and soon after were photographed frolicking on the Thames riverbank in front of the Houses of Parliament dressed in seaside get-up made from the kinds of goods sold cheaply to tourists as souvenirs of London. Much of their work momentarily celebrated an imaginative reworking of the capital as a place of leisure and pleasure, but it also managed quietly to mock the idea of how to market London fashion internationally.

The presentation of chintz in the very first issue of the Condé Nast-published *World of Interiors* magazine in 1982 edited by Min Hogg did much to promote it as a crucial textile design for the 1980s. The main feature of the first issue was an article on the singer Bryan Ferry's new apartment in Chelsea, which caused a degree of consternation for revealing Roxy Music's singer to be an arch traditionalist rather than an arbiter of modern style. The expectation of a bachelor pad smattered with the effects of pop culture, or a French apartment with a grand piano tinkling in the corner (as some of his lyrics have pictured), were dismissed by a vision of what the editor described as a 'miniature stately home in a small studio flat in London'. The decorative scheme, designed by Nicholas Haslam, included two kinds of chintz, blue-and-white china and a marble fireplace.

Looking at photographs of the interior, one could not imagine the place to be a small studio, more a large formal room. The ingenuity of the scheme was that the proportions of the interior detailing had been beautifully scaled so that the symmetries and balance of a seemingly grand design were executed in a small and otherwise unsuitable space.

Mark & Syrie, St George's Church, London, 1984.

Crucial to this effect, of course, was the scale of the chintz. Ferry, like Crolla, had been art-school trained, in his case at Newcastle upon Tyne under Richard Hamilton in the late 1960s. His concern with surface and style as a means of projection for his persona claimed chintz and the Chelsea squire as a combination that led on effortlessly from exotic climes and safari jackets to 'These Foolish Things' and formal dress for dinner. The problem was that instead of looking as if it had been there for years, the chintz room looked more artificial than any of Ferry's other looks.

This was a problem that was not isolated to Ferry; it was just that he made it seem more glaringly obvious. Peter York claimed that manufacturers of chintz 'would be ruined if they ever admitted that anyone called a designer, anyone who looked, thought, talked or wrote like one, went anywhere near those floral patterns. Those rosy bowers just grew there.'[7] And this was the problem with using chintz for the interior in the 1980s: it just looked as if it had always been there. There was no sense of it being thought of as postmodern, since you saw only the clouded varnish of historicism.

The exception to this rule was if you set it against a modern classic, as demonstrated by an advertisement of 1986 for Liberty's department store featuring the design consultant Stephen Bayley, who was director of the Boilerhouse Project at the V&A. In the ad Bayley sits on a Le Corbusier Grand Confort sofa from 1928, which bears a re-scaled William Morris floral print cushion made by Liberty's. This was how you made the historical floral print work in an interior design situation, by getting it to bear its postmodern credentials through the manipulation of scale.

This is also the very reason why Crolla shirts stood out, for the mischievous use of another designer's work. This concept, more widely known as appropriation, was to become a crucial practice of postmodern photography in the period, most notably in the work of the American artists Sherrie Levine and Richard Prince. As artists they were concerned with undermining concepts of authenticity by questioning the political legitimacy of authorship within the art medium of photography. This take-without-asking approach does have a precedent in the punk practice of detournement, but this particular kind of appropri-ation was never cheaply reproduced to point to the fact that it had been taken. It was often produced to similarly high standards, gaining its status through stealth. The referencing of these ideas in British graphic design by Peter Saville is worth consideration since it also employs a floral motif.

Saville's act of appropriation for the New Order Album *Power, Corruption & Lies* of 1983 was to take a still-life oil painting of flowers by the nineteenth-century French painter Henri Fantin-Latour and present it cropped to the square dimensions of the album sleeve. What was notable about the design was that it did not bear the title or the album or the artist on the cover. By doing this it was also a rework-ing of Richard Hamilton's concept for the Beatles' White album, but instead of standing out from other covers because there was nothing to see, Saville's design stood out for being an insertion of a decorative style that was the opposite of what most record sleeves looked like at the time. Hamilton's white album was important for the way in which it presented each record with its own edition number, borrow-ing the idea from the fine art principle of numbering an editioned work, whereas Saville's design borrowed an idea from fine art dis-course that was intent on making the edition as reproducible as pos-sible without any guarantee of authenticity. For Saville, the authenti-city lay in how you timed the appearance of the appropriation. As he later recounted:

> Of course, the whole point with appropriation is knowing what to do and when. Try to find the graphic design house that didn't have a Bauhaus book on its coffee table by the mid-1980s – you wouldn't have found one in 1978 or 1979. In 1983, when I put flowers on the cover of Power, Corruption & Lies, we hadn't seen flowers in pop culture since the 1960s. But fashion designer Scott Crolla was buying Sanderson fabric and Georgina Godley was running it up into dresses and there was this buzz about Flower Power coming back.[8]

But this was not to be the return of flower power as a free commodity, but as one that would remain without price because it was not paid for, a commodity whose value would reside only in its capacity for exchange. And it flaunted the fact that it had been lifted. In Saville's design the colour code bar printed at the top right corner of the cover is the indication that it is a unique image lifted for mass reproduction – an image of the past hijacked for the commercial needs of a product that needed an identity to sell itself.

Much of the criticism of postmodern design practice centres on the supposed emptiness of pastiche and the ethics of appropriation when using cultural history as a source. But Saville's and Crolla's appropriations are rooted by the geographical specificity of where they are drawn from in London. They are redolent of the reconquest of space in the city through the re-enchantment of place by the individual. They serve to demonstrate the urban roaming of a generation keen to find their own histories. For the use of the Fantin-Latour surely conjures afternoons spent in the National Gallery visiting the nineteenth-century European galleries where the original hangs, and the use of the Sanderson fabric evokes a walk along the rose-blossomed paths in the Physic Garden at Chelsea and a trip to the Chelsea Gardener. Both examples demonstrate the visual affluence afforded the art-school graduate in taking images from the city for their own ideas about fashionable identity.

Crolla's own shop on Dover Street very much traded on its historical associations, be it in the fact that Rupert Lycett Green had his menswear shop, Blades, there in the 1960s, or that the ICA had premises there in the 1950s; or even that Solomon's, the florists famous for their blooms for suit buttonholes, traded there in the 1930s. As a designer Crolla was adept at reclaiming the symbolic archaeology of an area by placing it in his own universe of connection that informed his designs. You could go so far as to say that the art-school graduates of the 1980s were not so much interested in acting like 'the flowers in your dustbin'– the phrase that defined the punks of the late 1970s – but instead drew upon the ideas found in the rose-bowl of the previous century.

The cultural figure from which both these models derive much of their spirit is the swagger of the dandy. Flowers were long associated with dandies, whether in the modernity of Baudelaire's collection of poems *Les Fleurs du mal* (1857) or in Oscar Wilde's popular identification in the 1890s by his holding of a daffodil. The shock that they posed in their time was in the way that they challenged the accepted codes of masculinity through gender ambiguity and an exploration of the themes of decadence. The New Romantics rekindled much of this in the early 1980s, lacing it with a slightly harder Weimar-inspired edge. But their nightly parading in fancy dress and make-up was more about masquerade than any kind of real challenge to masculinity. The floral challenge originated by the dandies find their re-expression in the 1980s in Morrissey, the stage persona of Stephen Patrick Morrissey.

Although Morrissey was not from London and had no art-school education, his impact on the sensibilities of the art-school graduate of the 1980s is without question. The record sleeves for his band The Smiths bore 'cover stars' drawn from a rich reference of literary and artistic camp from the recent past, whether Jean Marais, Joe Dallesandro or Yootha Joyce. Their reproduction, often in black and white or two-colour printing, made them as startling on the record shelves as Saville's use of past images. But it was in his use of flowers as a stage prop and accessory for his performing outfits that made this idea explicit. It is thought that Morrissey had originally wanted to perform holding liliums, the flowers that Oscar Wilde used while a student to perfume his quarters, but their prohibitive expense caused him to resort to gladioli and the occasional daffodil. The ardent quality of his lyrics, mapping a cultural terrain of Manchester brightly speckled with sardonic wit, made The Smiths' concerts in London seem like a strange echo back to Wilde's American tour of the 1890s, where the stage was recreated as the salon and guests would gather to hear proclamations about strange ways and unfamiliar places.

Morrissey's London fans were legion, and they could be easily spotted by the way they sported flowers hanging from the back pocket of their jeans, copying their idol. The popularity of Crolla's chintz clothing was in many ways an extension of this chain of association, but the problem in this was that few clothes bore the Crolla label, since they were by and large copies of the look sold on the high street. In an interview for I-D magazine in 1985, Crolla claimed the copying as

> good for you in the sense that it appears to be influential – but the copiers are the worst people in the world. I don't consider it flattering that someone rips-off my ideas, I think It's a really sad state of affairs that people work like that . . . people like Warehouse have no merit at all. Their criterion is that they are producing the same goods for wider market at cheaper prices . . . but that's dilution of an idea. We could go into mass production but we're just not interested in that. The fashion industry is just like any other – completely philistine and out to make as much money as possible . . . So there's no point continuing with something that is being plundered so much . . . it could go any way at the moment.[9]

Unfortunately for Crolla, the reproducibility of his appropriation was not something he could profit from, and it seems that, within fashion, appropriation and plundering were clearly different things. He continued his designing, turning to Indian silks heavily embroidered with gold thread, which were recently described by Colin McDowell as 'part-eighteenth-century, part-thirties-Colonialist and remarkably similar in spirit to the dress of the swinging sixties pop world'.[10] Their success, though, was short-lived, and the business soon disbanded.

For many London fashion designers within the period, the appeal of craft-based production on a single-outlet scale was much more appealing than the uniformity of mass production. They were happier working in the garden than the workshop and they cultivated an image of themselves that was just as rare and exotic as the blooms that they played with in their designs. Crolla's shirt design now seems like a souvenir to the re-imagination of London in the 1980s; it remains as if a memento of a flower pressed from a time gone by.

The timeliness of Crolla's contribution to fashion was unwittingly acknowledged in the year that it bloomed – in 1985 a new breed of rose was created, characterized by apricot blooms. It was named 'Chelsea'. At around the same time another menswear designer opened a shop in Covent Garden and his business grew into a global brand. Paul Smith continues to produce a floral shirt each season and the symbolic heart of his business remains in the first shop he opened in London – still trading today – on Floral Street.

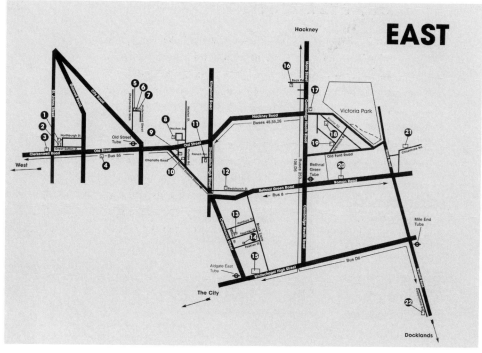

East London Gallery Guide, leaflet map, late 1990s.

CHAPTER EIGHT

The final chapter shifts upon London's oppositional axis – from West End to East End – and charts how the bounty of the garden withers across this distance and divide, transmuting into a wasteland. By the end of the 1980s, creative practitioners visited the idea of the garden as an aesthetic and spatial principle in London less and less. Those possessed of a 'special kind of city knowledge' were now more interested in the flip side of the equation: in the kind of areas that were abandoned and overgrown, but where deprivation was not experienced without a small sense of delight. It deals with the rearticulation of the East End as a setting for fashionable identities in the 1990s and scrutinizes the dissonance between this and an earlier vision of the area made in 1984.

In 1984 the artist Stephen Willats produced a piece of work that concentrated on the life of the fashion designer and notable night clubber Leigh Bowery, who had recently moved into a council block of flats off the Commercial Road in the East End of London with his friend Trojan. Bowery and Trojan were fêted at the time for their weekly appearance at the now legendary West End nightclub, Taboo, where their outfits brought the illogical to new extremes.

Willats's artwork is titled *What Is He Trying To Get At? Where Does He Want To Go?* and consists of two photographic panels depicting the block of flats by day and by night over which were collaged objects, images and written sentiments that defined Bowery and the things that surrounded him in his private world at these two distinct and separate times. The division between day and night was further evoked in the piece by a breeze-block column painted in Dayglo colours that separated the two panels, contributed by Bowery at the artist's request.

The artwork formed part of a broader enquiry established by Willats in the mid-1980s, which was concerned with the built architectural environment and how individual expression is conditioned by it. His work considered the relative impossibility of an individual being able to change or challenge the built metropolitan environment in which they live; and it documented the way in which the physical surfaces of the city impress themselves upon more private and individual surfaces, which the artist recorded with anthropological zeal. He became fascinated with those people who operated on the fringes, more interested in night than day, who were alienated from normality per se; but who lived, it seemed, in a manner far more striking than what might be thought of as everyday. In working against the rhythms of the everyday, they proposed an ingenious resistance to the radiations of the city's physical fabric, but a resistance that was very much informed by the metropolitan core of London's nightlife.

For a person like Bowery, it was in articulating the difference between the exotic and the mundane, in how the transitory and hedonistic experience of the night is underscored by the organized practicalities of a home and creative space in the day. For without the feasibility of the day, you could not have the slipperiness of the night. In interviews conducted to

Stephen Willats, *What Is He Trying To Get At? Where Does He Want To Go?*, 1984.

support the artwork, much is made of the capsule-like qualities of living in a high-rise flat – set within, yet distanced from everyday reality. Bowery was to liken it to a spaceship, 'hovering above reality', and illustrated the point by drawing one on the artwork in the style of Keith Haring.

At one stage in the interview Willats asked Bowery: 'Does being poor at the moment make you even more creative and more ingenious?' To which Bowery replied:

> Maybe more resourceful. If I had more money I'm sure I could do even more, but this way, the options aren't so great and so I

suppose resourcefulness is a sign of the times as well, when you have to. For us, it's how I wanted to use shag pile carpet, but instead we're using the cheapest fun fur I can get, but I think the effect will be more interesting and also, perhaps it says something about the time I bought it.[1]

Even though Bowery may well have been financially poor at this time, his ingenuity lay in transforming lowly materials bought from the locale into desirable statements of fashion. This led him to be courted by the New York club impresario and boutique owner Susanne Bartsch, whose New York fashion shows were instrumental in awakening the international fashion press to the creativity of London fashion in the mid-1980s. The collection that Bowery produced for her, entitled 'Pakis in Outer Space', ended up by heavily incorporating 'the cheapest fun fur', which they used for their interior (offset by Star Trek wallpaper), and the styling of the blue face paint and Asian jewellery that accompanied the collection is evident in the photographs of Bowery applied to Willats's artwork.

The cheap Indian grooming products and jewellery were bought from the shops of Brick Lane, which had begun to be colonized by the Bangladeshi community, while the fun fur was more a cheap tribute to the low-end fabric warehouses and sweat shops that still defined the trade of the area. (The outfits would later be used in Michael Clark's production of *The Fall* with set design based on paintings by Trojan that hung in the flat.) In being poor, Bowery constructed an excessive sensibility that was drawn from the everyday but distanced from its reality by its reconfiguration.

The artists Gilbert and George were also adept at realizing this community within the rigid grid formats of their large-scale photographic artworks constructed in the studio of their Georgian house on Fournier Street, just off Brick Lane. Through a formal visual language not dissimilar to the kind used by Willats, their style of documentation also enforced an aesthetic technique of distancing from the locale. These works by Gilbert and George and Willats presented the neglected and poor landscape of the East End through artistic eyes as a bountiful wasteland, rich in scope for transformation, with its deprivation reconfigured as a creative constraint.

As artistic statements about London in the 1980s, they are at odds with the vision of London as a Garden presented in the last chapter. But just like the imaginaries of the late nineteenth century who valorized the West End while demonizing the East, the West End of the 1980s was seen to blossom, while the East End decayed. This neglect was later redressed in the 1990s through the processes of gentrification that we will come to consider, but this vision of the East End as a creative wasteland remained persistent as an urban imaginary.

In 1996, at a time when the creativity of London in this decade was at a highpoint (and just before it was labelled 'Cool Britannia' by the British press), Willats's artwork from 1984 was re-exhibited at a summer show at the Lisson Gallery showing the work of a number of Young British Artists, and was also documented in the artist's monograph *Between Buildings and People* published in the same year. The resurfacing of this piece in the cultural landscape of the 1990s was perhaps in tribute to the recent death of Leigh Bowery, in 1994, and his ascendancy as a seminal figure of the London nightscape and art scene.

The display of this work was timely because contained within it are the features of creativity in the East End of London in the 1990s. First, it identifies the East End of London as a concrete and bleak post-war environment that forsakes the whimsical nostalgia for a working-class brick-built community of old. Secondly, it presents the area as a home to artists and offers itself as a means of creativity that is bountiful in cheap materials; and thirdly it communicates this chiefly through the medium of photography.

The only difference between the values of the artwork of 1984 and those of the 1990s lay in their geographical situation of an artistic life. For Bowery, his East End days were the unremarkable and unseen flipside to the fantastic notoriety of his West End nights, and Willats's artwork demonstrates this as a polarity in black and white. One can claim Bowery as a West End figure, even though he always lived in the East End, since it was only in the West End that you saw him, as he wanted you to see him. The extreme costumes he designed in which to go clubbing became so revered that they gained Bowery his own West End art exhibition in 1988 at the Anthony d'Offay Gallery, where he posed in the gallery as a living picture. Never one to shy from the use of a flesh-coloured body stocking, the daily presentation was a fitting homage to the Living Picture presentations on the Variety Theatre stages of the early twentieth century. Bowery later realized the chance to become the subject of an actual painting by becoming a celebrated model of the painter Lucian Freud in his Kensington studio, although for this role he regularly posed naked.

The difference in the creative culture of the 1990s in London is that the West End never really figured in the definition of an artistic life, since it consistently remained in the East End. On a very basic level of comparison, if you wanted to be someone like Bowery in the 1990s you no longer needed to go to the West End for galleries or clubs or even to be noticed, because everyone was doing it or looking for it in the East End.

While artists had long frequented the East End, the recession of the early 1990s afforded them new prospects. Light industrial spaces intended for businesses were now turned over to them as cheap live-work spaces or spaces in which to exhibit, and this forged a new influx of young creative practitioners into Hoxton, an area of east-central London that, had the economy of the 1980s continued unabated, would have been razed to extend the business complex of Broadgate that lies to the north of Liverpool Street Station.

And their position on the oppositional axis of East and West London became the means by which they could assert their new order: so the warehouse spaces of the East End and beyond became the spaces in which young artists challenged the West End galleries of Cork Street; or, as a further example, the alternative off-schedule East End venue became a space in which young fashion designers started to challenge the tents at South Kensington erected for the London Fashion Week. Scale was to become an important factor in these challenges, for at the *East Country Yard Show* (1990) curated by Sarah Lucas and Henry Bond, each artist showed in 20,000 square feet of space; Hussein Chalayan's fashion presentations at the Atlantis space in Brick Lane commanded over 14,000 square feet alone.

The group show at the Lisson Gallery (actually on the outskirts of the West End) in 1996 that featured Willats's piece was evidence of a new generation of East End artists that had begun to make similar claims about the relationship between the engrained anonymity of the urban environment and the way its debris could project something about an individual's identity as a city dweller. But rather than the East End of Whitechapel and Commercial Street of Bowery's day, many of these younger artists now centred on Shoreditch and Commercial Road. Joshua Compston's activities from his premises on Charlotte Road, particularly his two *Fête Worse than Death* events held in Hoxton Square, did much to publicize the reclaiming of the area by a new breed of artists who were not so much interested in distancing strategies, but in the participatory and inclusive qualities of artistic production. Leigh Bowery was to lend his own technical flare for these carnivalesque pageants, famously painting Angus Fairhurst's and Damien Hirst's faces as clowns for their double act, which included a peek for 50p at their genitalia, shaved and painted yellow with pink spots at Bowery's insistence.

The British style press quickly picked upon the fashionability of these events. *The Face* magazine commissioned an art special issue in 1996 that featured Gary Hume's *Jam Boots*, first featured at Compston's fête as the image for the invitation. Here, ingenuity from the position of poverty does not transform, but celebrates the poverty of materials through incongruity. The jam remains the cheap kind, the bread processed, sliced and white. Although supposedly mocking the fashionable idea of style constructed from the everyday, or style as sustenance, the boots are presented knowingly and mockingly as fashionable objects of desire.

Although they may have appeared seemingly resistant to the mechanics of fashion, the Young British Artists, as they were to be known, were more than self-conscious about fashionability and were adept at the language of presentation and channels of dissemination. The central role that the imagery of the style press would play in shaping this new aesthetic, for both artists and photographers, is best illustrated by returning to the depiction of Bowery by Willats.

Looking at a strip of photographs in Willats's book of 1996 that documents the artwork, Bowery is inserted as a made-up creature of the

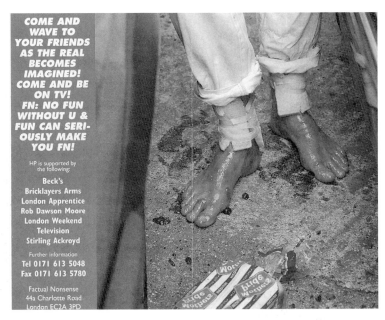

COME AND
WAVE TO
YOUR FRIENDS
AS THE REAL
BECOMES
IMAGINED!
COME AND BE
ON TV!
FN: NO FUN
WITHOUT U &
FUN CAN SERI-
OUSLY MAKE
YOU FN!

HP is supported by
the following:

**Beck's
Bricklayers Arms
London Apprentice
Rob Dawson Moore
London Weekend
Television
Stirling Ackroyd**

Further information
**Tel 0171 613 5048
Fax 0171 613 5780**

Factual Nonsense
44a Charlotte Road
London EC2A 3PD

Gary Hume, *Jam Boots*, 1995, on a poster for a Factual Nonsense event in Hoxton Square, Shoreditch, 1995.

night. He appears set between bleak shots of the view from his flat of the city, the communal corridor to the lifts, an outside view of the block and an image of Bowery without make-up staring wistfully out of the window in the cold light of day. The mundane quality of the photographs that hem Bowery in when dressed for the evening were meant to underline by contrast the bare logic of his existence in the East End block of flats. What they signalled in 1996 was how fashionable this sense of being informed by these bare, architectural surfaces had become, at the expense of the ingenious and elaborate costumes. The laboured performances of the night were abandoned in this new aesthetic for a nonchalance that could say something about the everyday. It favoured the cold light of day, but the reality it proposed was in fact just as elaborately constructed as one of Bowery's costumes.

Much of this new aesthetic was forged in editorial fashion photography, by those who wanted to reject unreachable visions of glamour

LB Well, I've never got enough money to do, you know, all the things I want to do, but that's good in a way because I actually become resourceful. Like, for example, that shag pile, we're going to replace it with something even better, like this beautiful fun fur.

SW I suppose we're talking about aggravation from neighbours and things but do you get any general aggravation from people?
LB Oh, you get ups and downs. I mean, it happens all the time. I'm always meeting people as well, because of the way I look people come up to me, so you quickly learn what people are like, what you're going to expect from them and what they'll expect from you and so you can handle things like that quite subtly.

16 April 1984

SW Right, these are just some questions that emerged from looking at the transcripts of the first tape we made together. One of the things that interested me was whether you felt that these days the only way to get a place like you've got is to do something fairly desperate, you know, that's the only way you can get something out of the council?
LB I suppose you do get it if you're prepared to wait, but we weren't, we just wanted it straight away. We're always a bit eager to get things done like red tape and things like that is pointless, so we tried to think of the fastest way we could, like burning our front door down and pretending we were being harassed all the time.

SW Now you're in here, are you trying to create a special atmosphere inside the place?
LB Well, I suppose, because the government and society's got those sort of priorities, yes, I do want to create something where you can think the way I do that's completely separate from it, you know, in a way a bit like an escape from all the pressures I normally feel, like when I turn the TV on I see them again, but the environment's a bit like a capsule or something, sort of separate.

but because I'm so into my appearance all the time they seem a bit superfluous, so I stick with things I can use, like plates and cups and things that I use all the time. I'm quite into them because I see them or I like them to be pleasing to me. We're going to get this china, just plain white china from Woolworths and you can buy these dyes and things you paint on to it, leave them to dry for forty-eight hours or something in an airing cupboard and the design stays on. They'll be quite nice objects to look at and I'll be using them all the time, but objects like – oh I can't imagine – oh it's just the objects that which are immediately around me that interest me.

SW So objects are like tools that you need?
LB I do like having nice tools, this standard of my work's better when I've got the proper things to use. I like my machines when they're running smoothly and I've got a good stitch; that is really pleasing. Once upon a time I couldn't care less, but now I feel really happy when they're working, 'cos that's all buggered up at the moment.

SW Finally, does being poor at the moment, make you even more creative and more ingenious?
LB Maybe more resourceful. If I had more money I'm sure I could do even more, but this way, the options aren't so great and so I suppose resourcefulness is a sign of the times as well, when you have to. For us it's how I wanted to use shag pile carpet, but instead we're using the cheapest fun fur I can get, but I think the effect will be more interesting and also, perhaps it says something about the time I bought it.

Stephen Willats, preparatory works for *What Is He Trying To Get At? Where Does He Want To Go?*, 1984, as they appear in his *Between Buildings and People* (1996).

and reflect a vision of reality. Yet in working so closely with reality, the medium succeeded in making reality obsolete through its very replication. In moving beyond the traditional non-space of studio-based fashion photography shot against a white backdrop, this fashioned reality depicted the streets and spaces of the city. The images did not depict them literally – only half recognizably – in order that the specificity of time and space was veiled by a patina that spoke of an authentic kind of metropolitan experience.

The realism found in these photographs was often in the difference between what was expected of them in the context of a magazine and what they failed to deliver; conventionally fashionable clothes were not their concern, or if they were, the point was not to render them as such. This photographic 'look' not only attempted to resist the wider revolutions of consumerism, but also the seamless aesthetic of the newly developed digitally enhanced image. The wishful location of this non-place in the East End of London became the means by which the fantasy of something being reclaimed, in more than one sense of the word, could take place. The urban imaginary of the East End as a wasteland was found in the casual neglect of many of the settings used in this new kind of editorial fashion photography, which saw fancy in the disregarded interior, and which revelled in the delinquency of the individual and in the slack nihilism of a gesture. Cheap hotel rooms with faded furnishing fabrics, rain-stained windows and greasy headboards were recast as introspective spaces that reflected the subject's state of mind. In their decaying state, these places could be read as architectural metaphors for psychological paralysis.

In an early example, *London Hotel Guest* (1993) by Donald Milne, a girl sits on a bed adjusting the sleeve of her dress in a somewhat uncomfortable position while straining to watch a television positioned awkwardly high in the corner of the room. The uncared-for interior is somewhat at odds with the girl, and the image is further unsettled by the reflection of the girl's shoulder and arm in the mirror of the cheap dressing table. Although the scene should be cast as private, the presence of the photographer in the image – while not overly voyeuristic – claims the space and its banal surfaces not as private, not even public, but somehow as shared. And this shared quality also becomes the trigger for the inclination a certain kind of loneliness and vulnerability, but one that is cast as a fantasy, or rather, a distraction.

When not set in an interior, this new kind of fashion photography often used the city street as a setting. What was unusual about these kinds of images was how they maintained a shared sense of the public and private in the desire to etch personal patinas onto the blank surfaces of the street. This can be evidenced in the photograph *Karen Ferrari, London 1992* by Juergen Teller. Here, the model is photographed from above as she wanders aimlessly towards a dead end in the grounds of a council estate familiar to many areas of inner-city London. She

Donald Milne, *London Hotel Guest*, 1993.

wears nothing but a pair of white jeans that are too long for her legs, marked brown at the hems from wandering across the rain-soaked pavements, whilst she tilts her head in dislocation. While the pose itself is not particularly new, the private mood of introspection would be more appropriate in an interior situation, staring into a dressing mirror in a bedroom rather than a brick wall on a communal path.

Juergen Teller, *Karen Ferrari*, London, 1992.

Although surreal displacement is a credited technique in fashion photography, here it is abandoned for derangement. The muddied jeans echo the corroded steel doors of the generator room, while the washing lines in the back gardens beyond the dividing wall speak of domesticity abandoned.

As a figure in the city the model does not stroll like the *flâneur*, taking pleasure in the visual spectatorship of the metropolitan environment, nor does she bear the mask of reserve that Simmel claimed as essential to navigation and sanity as a city dweller. Rather, she appears as the kind of person that one sees everyday in London whose behaviour remains indecipherable by aimless meandering. This is not the resistance to everyday life practised by Leigh Bowery through choice and exoticism, but one presented through indifference and disinterestedness: a kind of defiant unconcern, potent in its ability to retain its attractiveness when commodified as an image. In its abandoning of consumerism the image represents the ideas shared by many of those creating fashion photography at this time in London: that fashion was at its most interesting in a state of stasis, at a dead end.

This in turn quickly became the desirable visual language to sell fashion in advertising campaigns, even if the image was at odds with what it was intending to promote. A good example of this is a later range of images by Teller for an advertising campaign for Jigsaw Menswear in 1997. They describe an urban landscape predominantly of concrete in which the male model is posed in scenes that are structured to appear violent. Like a stunt double the model tumbles down corridor steps as if thrown; he smashes through a windowpane or dives to the floor with his suit on fire. A group of images show him standing at the edge of a tower block rooftop, diving off this position, falling through mid-air and then lying face-down on the ground.

The campaign bore strong art-historical references, informed by the staged photographs of Yves Klein jumping off a building and his performances in blow-torching canvases; another reference was the surreal scene of a man riding a bicycle lying in the road in Luis Bunuel's and Salvador Dalí's film *Un chien andalou* (1929). The themes of violence and death were not particularly new for fashion photography at this point, but considered as a statement on the individual and their relationship to the city the troubled images are quite revealing.

In the image of a man wearing a suit lying face-down on a concrete floor he appears as if he had just committed suicide. The lifelessness of the body seems to reflect on the inorganic quality of the environment where nothing seems to grow, while the perversity of using the harrowing imagery of suicide to sell something desirable is suggestive of despair. What is perhaps more perverse is that the man could be mistaken for embracing the floor that he lies on, as if wishing passionately to connect with this concrete surface, with what is arguably construed as an urban wasteland.

As a vision of a wasteland it is very much in keeping with the sentiments expressed in T. S. Eliot's poem of the same name of 1922, which presents the city of London as a scene of paralysis as its central theme:

> What are the roots that clutch, what branches grow
> Out of this stony rubbish? Son of man,
> You cannot say, or guess, for you know only
> A heap of broken images . . . [2]

Eliot's poem claims modern London as a wasteland and charts a soul in despair, lost in a terrain of spiritual drought. It sets the stagnation of the present against the fecundity of the past, but suggests through 'the heap of broken images' that all we have of the past is in fragmented form and that our hope of continuity is as disconnected as the fragmentary experience of modern life. Much of the poem describes the wasteland of London as a barren landscape that is haunted by the voices of the past held in its layers of subterranean sediment.

Teller's images for the advertising campaign can also be read as a heap of broken images, as representing the broken body of a soul in despair, unable to cope with the experience of living in the city by being unable to connect with its hard surfaces. The crucial difference in this comparison, though, is that the images fail to represent any sense of the past as 'a heap of broken images'. The only indicator of the past is in the concrete surfaces of the post-war housing blocks

that the shoot was staged in, textured and weather-beaten by the rav-
ages of time.

The notion of citing personal experience within impersonal surfaces
was explored by a number of artists based in the East End at this point.
They used discarded objects and broken materials, particularly those
found in the street, as the source material for exploration. The curator
Emma Dexter described this transformation of rubbish into art as offering 'a patina or history combined with the lure of erasure' and she identified this dialectic as being particular to London as a creative capital.[3]

Gary Hume's early paintings are a case in point. *Dolphin Painting One*
(1991) is a painting in imitation of the double doors found in the corridors of St Bartholomew's Hospital in Smithfield. In reproducing the
doors in paint, Hume intensified the gloss by applying numerous
coats to its surface, mimicking the accumulation of paint layers that
the actual doors in the hospital had received over time. The painting,
then, is about the history of the doors and the history of the people
who have experienced them. In being repainted, their patinas were
erased but they remained sedimented under a seemingly blank surface.
In a strange way their composition (as doors and as a painting) is not
unlike the paradox in the relationship between the disconnected present and the layered past in Eliot's poem. Further, just like the poem
they deal in the specificity of a London landmark, but one that points to
a universal theme. Hume underlines this in his reason for choosing the
particular hospital doors to copy: 'I didn't want them to have class references; grand verses council flat . . . or to show aspiration and design
consciousness. So I chose the kind of doors that we all go through at one
time or another.'[4]

The painting, then, is suggestive of a personal and emotional investment experienced by many in a single set of doors that offer no way of
marking that relation, but persist in the memory of that experience. As
a surface it represents the thin line between the public and the private
in the city; and it replicates a shared sense of vulnerability under a
seemingly blank and anonymous modernity.

In many ways Hume's painting mourns the rejection of memory in
the man-made environments that were the product of the modernist

Gary Hume, *Dolphin V*, 1991, gloss paint on two MDF panels.

programme; but it also maintains the wish to secrete emotions, or etch them in their surfaces. As an idea, this was perhaps most poetically expressed in the objects cast by the artist Rachel Whiteread, formed from the inverted space of abandoned objects. Her sculptures of mattresses and baths bore the physical traces of a prior relationship with a range of individuals, whilst retaining a sense of a thing cast off and discarded in the neglected corners of the city. As artworks they pose as ghosts of memories about those objects given form and made material.

Tim Noble and Sue Webster, *Dirty White Trash (with Gulls)*, 1998, rubbish, seagulls, projector.

This strategy of transforming a secondary material culture of the lost and found reached its apotheosis in the work of Tim Noble and Sue Webster, who had become famous for the studio they rented on Rivington Street in Shoreditch. Their later work addressed the urban experience of living as artists in the East End, formed from the jetsam and flotsam of litter that was a perennial feature of the unkempt streets. *Dirty White Trash (with Gulls)* took a seemingly artless pile of rubbish, which, when illuminated from behind, cast a perfect silhouette on the opposite wall of a scene depicting the artists sharing a cigarette and a glass of wine on a hillock, while at its edge seagulls fight over discarded scraps.

In this piece the materials that chart the ebb and flow of movement along the street become the means by which identity and place can be fixed. Yet the Arcadia projected remains a temporary illumination, a trick of the eye that is pleasurable rather than participatory. The artwork was a wry comment on those who regularly came to the East End to witness everything that the British press had written about the area, only to find run-down light-industrial buildings and swirling rubbish.

More than the other two artists discussed, Noble and Webster align themselves in the artwork with the lot of the rag-and-bone man. He is a figure who haunts the imagination of the East End, collecting, sifting and sorting all that is discarded before turning it into profit and reward. Another figure that is undeniably similar to him is the nineteenth-century rag picker, who performs the same duties but concentrates on clothes. Caroline Evans identified him in the writings of Walter Benjamin as a metaphorical figure for fashion designers in the 1990s.[5] Like the rag picker she claimed them as being particularly adept at using the broken images of the past as source material for their creativity in the present.

The difference between them, though, is that the rag picker transforms his materials into money, whereas fashion creators turn them into images that have their own kind of currency (hoping these images will eventually pay dividends in the market). It is relatively easy to extend this argument to the artists and photographers I am dealing with, since they are all concerned with creating images that define the notion of spectacle, be it an installation, a fashion show or a photographic image. What I suppose defines much of the work I have been discussing is its strange sense of place located in the East End.

Earlier I raised the idea that the East End came into focus in the 1990s as the locus for creativity and display at the expense of the West End. It became celebrated as a wasteland bountiful in materials, ripe for artistic transformation, and its status was maintained as a non-place in opposition to the well-defined status of the West End as the place of spectacle and pleasure. In this construct, the East End offered itself as the wasteland at the side of the attraction that is the West End. As such, it was in keeping with the status of Marc Auge's work of the non-places of urban culture such as shopping malls and airport departure lounges. Auge's theories had a particular impact on the production of photography imagery in the period and it helped shape the non-place of the East End as a spectacle that defined 'place' by its cultural centrality.

What was curious about this, though, was the persistence in the values held in the depiction of liminal spaces and casual neglect, placed at the interface of the public and private. The projection of reality that this kind of image-making sought was not intended to jolt the viewer, but instead offer a contemplative lull, a representation of an absorbed introspection for contemplation. In the sense of appearing as if waiting for something to happen, this imagery bears relation to the writings of Siegfried Kracauer. In his study of the structural qualities of modernity in his native 1920s Berlin, Kracauer used the spatial order of the hotel lobby to make sense of everyday life through its difference from the qualities of a church and the relation it bears to its congregation. Seeing modern life as somehow meaningless in its anonymous transactions, Kracauer likened it to a hotel for the fact that it 'appears as a place of silence, avoided eye contact, distant relations, unreality, anonymity and insubstantial aesthetics'.[6] He was very much concerned with the quality of detachment that the hotel lobby achieved from everyday reality; in the way that it offered a contemplative recourse from the everyday, but not an escape from it.

The photographs of Hannah Starkey, which came to prominence at the end of the 1990s, evoke many of Kracauer's themes. As images they are significant because they demonstrate the interplay between fashion magazine publishing, new kinds of photography and the exhibition of art that came about at this time. On first impressions her work seems to be social documentary, but it is in fact traded as art. Further, Starkey produced a number of commissions for *Vogue Hommes International* and other style magazines in the late 1990s. The juncture between art and fashion that Starkey's work seems to occupy has come to inform many of the themes of boredom and disconnection in the images, and in turn helps to illuminate the structure of feeling and its dissemination particular to the period.

Hannah Starkey, *It's a God's life. Down to earth but infinitely just the same. Passing through. Heaven can wait*, in *Vogue Hommes International*, spring/summer 1999.

The photographic historian Val Williams has written that there is 'nothing consoling about Hannah Starkey's cool gaze at the city, no vitality, no connection', even though her subjects are often the young and fashionable.[7] In photographs published in *Vogue Hommes International* in spring–summer 1999, Starkey used a variety of situations based in London (some credited, some not) to create a fashion spread about the nature of disconnection in the metropolis.

A crucial image is a photograph of a girl standing at a coat-check counter at the Connaught Hotel in Mayfair. The fashionable clothes she wears are construed as her work uniform, yet she looks far from wanting to serve anyone. In the photograph Starkey suggests that participation in the hotel lobby condition is a necessary condition of youth culture, a uniform that has to be worn at the expense of the individual; as something that has to be worked at, as something equal to the condition of labour.

This representation of indifference does, of course, have a historical precedent in the concept of alienation as a response to increased industrialization and urbanization in the nineteenth century. Further, *ennui* as an existential derelict pose established the condition as capable of stylization in the post-war period. But rather than appearing 'pretty vacant' in the agitated style of punk, these images bear a vacancy that, while remaining pretty, is without intent. As scenarios of boredom they are not expressive of vitality or movement, but what can be described as 'drift'.

This concept derives from the Situationists, who thought it a form of human behaviour informed by urban conditions of ambience and transience. It is not about a casual engagement with the city; rather, it is more about chance and a certain chaos, but not one that springs forth, but one that maintains a stillness and inertia in resistance to the pace of the city. The staged qualities of Starkey's photos underline this sense of stillness as a form of resistance. Her images suggest that the metropolis is the place where inertia can be understood as a means to resist the speed of the city and, in turn, the speed and indicators of fashion.

Another image by Starkey depicts a young couple seated in the window of a cab firm awaiting their journey. Its very stillness infers that the experience of waiting is more of a journey that the actual taxi ride. It privileges the cognitive mapping of the East End over the empirical mapping of its realities. It is the non-place over the destination. It is about the Soft City of Jonathan Raban's construction, rather than the Hard. It is the triumph of stillness over movement, imagination over change; but it produced an urban imaginary that in turn visually articulated the stasis of ambivalence. Directing the title of Stephen Willats's 1984 piece to the young people in Starkey's photograph, we can appreciate the importance that these unanswered questions would assume in the fashioning of the East End in the 1990s: 'What Are They Trying To Get At? Where Do They Want to Go?'

Hannah Starkey, *Untitled*, in *Vogue Hommes International*, spring/summer 1998.

REFERENCES

INTRODUCTION

1 Bob Stanley, 'The Naked City', *Guardian Friday Review* (21 November 2003), p. 10.
2 M. Christine Boyer, *The City of Collective Memory* (Cambridge, MA, and London, 1996), p. 442.
3 Caroline Evans, *Fashion at the Edge* (London, 2003), introduction.
4 Jonathan Raban, *Soft City* (London, 1974), p. 102.
5 Ibid., pp. 66–7.
6 Iain Chambers, 'Maps for the Metropolis: A Possible Guide to the Present', *Cultural Studies*, 1/1 (January 1987), p. 7.
7 Georg Simmel, 'Fashion', in *On Individuality and Social Forms*, ed. Donald N. Levine (Chicago, 1971), p. 303.
8 Michel de Certeau, *The Practice of Everyday Life* (Berkeley, CA, 1984), p. 93.
9 Steve Pile and Nigel Thrift, eds, *Mapping the Subject: Geographies of Cultural Transformation* (London, 1995), p. 1.
10 Raban, *Soft City*, p. 10.

CHAPTER ONE

1 Gambier Bolton, 'Pictures on the Human Skin', *Strand Magazine*, XIII (1897), p. 54.
2 Donald Fletcher, 'Tattooing among Civilized People', *Anthropological Society of Washington* (1882), p. 26.
3 Adolf Loos, 'Crime and Ornamentation', in *Modernism in Design*, ed. P. Greenhalgh (London, 1990), p. 19.
4 George Burchett, *Memoirs of a Tattooist* (London, 1958), p. 40.
5 Lynda Nead, *Victorian Babylon* (London, 2000), p. 3.
6 Burchett, *Memoirs of a Tattooist*, p. 105.
7 Bolton, 'Pictures on the Human Skin', p. 54.
8 Quoted in Toshio Watanabe, *High Victorian Japonisme* (Bern, 1991), p. 161.
9 Bolton, 'Pictures on the Human Skin', p. 54.
10 Ibid.
11 David Urquhart, *The Pillars of Hercules; or, A Narrative of Travels in Spain and Morocco* (London, 1848), p. v.
12 Karl Beckson , *London in the 1890s: A Cultural History* (New York and London, 1992), p. 264.

13   *Pall Mall Gazette* (1 May 1889), p. 2.
14   'The Gentle Art of Tattooing: The Fashionable Craze of Today', *The Tatler*, 126 (25 November 1903), p. 311.
15   Margot Mifflin, *Bodies of Subversion: A Secret History of Women and Tattoo* (New York, 1997), p. 22.
16   Playbill, Royal Acquarium, in Farini's Gallery, Farini's World of Wonders, 1882, Westminster City Archives, AO4A 1650.

CHAPTER TWO

1   Beresford Chancellor, *Wanderings in Piccadilly, Mayfair and Pall Mall* (London, 1908).
2   Cecil Beaton, *The Glass of Fashion* (London, 1954), p. xx.
3   Museum of London, 28.125/1–2.
4   Lady Duff Gordon, *Discretions and Indiscretions* (New York, 1932), p. 67.
5   Gilles Lipovetsky, *The Empire of Fashion: Dressing Modern Democracy* (Princeton, NJ, 1994), p. 79.
6   Elinor Glyn, *Three Weeks* (London, 1907), pp. 85–6.
7   Meredith Etherington-Smith and Jeremy Pilcher, *The 'It' Girls: Lucy, Lady Duff Gordon, the Couturière 'Lucile' and Elinor Glyn* (London, 1986), p. 107.
8   Natalie Rothenstein, ed., *Four Hundred Years of Fashion* (London, 1984), p. 80.
9   Duff Gordon, *Discretions and Indiscretions*, p. 67.
10   Ed Lilley, 'Art, Fashion and the Nude', *Fashion Theory*, V/1 (March 2001), pp. 57–77.
11   *Saturday Review* (6 April 1895).
12   National Vigilance Association, pamphlet, 1904, p. v.
13   '*Tableaux vivants* at the Palace Theatre', *The Sketch* (28 March 1894), p. 482.
14   Louise Heilgers, 'Delightful Dresses at Daly's', *Play Pictorial*, X/61 (1907).
15   Etherington-Smith and Pilcher, *The 'It' Girls*, p. 57.
16   Duff Gordon, *Discretions and Indiscretions*, p. 278.

CHAPTER THREE

1   *Daily Mirror* (12 June 1936), p. 2.
2   *International Surrealist Bulletin*, 4 (June 1936), pp. 2–3.
3   *Surrealism in the 1930s*, transcript of a lecture by Eileen Agar at the Royal College of Art, March 1988.

4 Cecil Beaton's sketchbooks are in the Archive of Art and Design, London, ADD/1986/13.

5 Elsa Schiaparelli, *Shocking Life* (London, 1954), p. 46.

6 'A Midnight Draw', *Daily Star* (25 November 1937).

7 Eileen Agar, Manuscript for Autobiography, 2 January 1985, Tate Archive, 911.38.

8 Tristan Tzara, 'Of a Certain Automatism of Taste', *Le Minotaure*, III (1933), pp. 81–4.

9 Richard Martin, *Fashion & Surrealism* (London, 1988), pp. 11.

10 Eileen Agar, *A Look at My Life* (London, 1988), p. 19.

11 Roland Penrose, *Scrapbook, 1900–1981* (London, 1981), p. 60; Penrose's photographs of Surrealist albums are in the Conway Library, Courtauld Institute of Art, London (1848A).

12 *Daily Sketch*, undated cutting *c.*1937, Eileen Agar Archive, Tate Britain.

13 A. G. Thornton, 'Padded Wheelbarrow for the Drawing-Room: How Surrealism Strikes a Dustman', *Daily Star* (25 November 1937).

CHAPTER FOUR

1 In Daniel Farson, *The Gilded Gutter Life of Francis Bacon* (London, 1993), p. 132.

2 Michael Peppiatt, *Francis Bacon: Anatomy of an Enigma* (London, 1996), p. 206.

3 Ibid., p. 208.

4 Nigel Richardson, *Dog Days in Soho: One Man's Adventures in 1950s Bohemia* (London, 2000), preface.

5 *Studio Magazine* (August 1930), pp. 140–41.

6 Adrian Searle, 'This Too, Too Squalid Flesh', *The Guardian* (4 February 1998), p. 10.

7 John Berger, *About Looking* (New York, 1991), p. 119.

8 Peppiatt, *Francis Bacon*, p. 259.

9 *Keith Vaughan Diaries: Journals, 1939–1977* (London, 1989), p. 99 [27 January 1955].

10 David Sylvester, *Interviews with Francis Bacon* (London, 1975), p. 192.

11 In Farson, *The Gilded Gutter Life of Francis Bacon*, p. 40. See Michael Wishart, *High Diver* (London, 1977).

12 Farson, *The Gilded Gutter Life of Francis Bacon*, p. 129.

13 Stanley Jackson, *Indiscreet Guide to Soho* (London, 1946), p. 114.

14 'Meet the Spiv', *Tailor & Cutter* (15 August 1947), p. 561.

15 Julian Maclaren Ross, *Memoirs of the Forties* (London, 1965), p. 123.

16 Simon Roberts, 'Feeling Blighted', in *Waterstone's Guide to London*

17 Jackson, *Indiscreet Guide to Soho*, p. 114.
18 Institute of Contemporary Arts, London, debate , 11 March 1952.
19 Anonymous, 'Foreword', in John Deakin, *London Today* (London, 1949).
20 Farson, *The Gilded Gutter Life of Francis Bacon*, p. 49.
21 *Man about Town* (Spring 1956), p. 61.

CHAPTER FIVE

1 *Daily Telegraph* (30 April 1965).
2 Jonathan Green, *All Dressed Up* (London, 1998), p. 70.
3 Ibid., p. 86.
4 Christopher Booker, *The Neophiliacs* (London, 1969), p. 133.
5 *New York Herald Tribune* (20 October 1965).
6 *Queen* (October 1968).
7 *Daily Express* (16 April 1970).
8 *Queen* (July 1969).
9 Mary Quant, *Quant on Quant* (London, 1966), p. 80.
10 *Life Magazine* (July 1966).
11 *Daily Telegraph* (27 June 1966).
12 Jonathan Raban, *Soft City* (London, 1974), p. 66.
13 Nik Cohn, *Today There Are No Gentlemen* (Birkenhead, 1971), p. 118.
14 Green, *All Dressed Up*, p. 81.

CHAPTER SIX

1 *The London Weekend Show: Fashion and the King's Road*, London Weekend Television (31 July 1977).
2 Craig Bromberg, *The Wicked Ways of Malcolm McLaren* (London, 1991), pp. 41–2.
3 Dick Hebdige, *Subculture: The Meaning of Style* (London, 1988), p. 82.
4 Raphael Samuel, *Theatres of Memory* (London, 1994), pp. 92–3.
5 George Melly, *Revolt into Style: The Pop Arts in Britain* (London, 1972), p. 137.
6 Reyner Banham, 'All That Glitters Is Not Stainless', in *The Aspen Papers* (London, 1974), p. 351.
7 Corin Hughes-Stanton, 'What Comes After Carnaby Street', *Design Magazine*, no. 203 (February 1968), p. 42.
8 Philip Core, *Camp: The Lie That Tells the Truth* (London, 1984), p. 14.

9   'Is Bad Taste Such a Bad Thing?', British *Vogue* (June 1971), p. 144.

10   Deyan Sudjic in *Architectural Review* (September 1977), p. 45.

11   *An Endless Adventure . . . An Endless Passion . . . An Endless Banquet: A Situationist Scrapbook* (London, 1989), p. 10.

12   *The London Weekend Show: Fashion and the King's Road*, London Weekend Television (31 July 1977).

CHAPTER SEVEN

1   Peter York, *The Eighties* (London, 1993).

2   Caroline Evans and Minna Thornton, *Women and Fashion: A New Look* (London, 1989), p. 78.

3   Robert Venturi, *Leaving from Las Vegas* (Cambridge, MA, 1972).

4   Scott Crolla, email correspondence with the author.

5   Reginald Blunt, *The Wonderful Village: A Further Record of Some Famous Folk and Places by Chelsea Reach* (London, 1918), p. xx.

6   Chelsea Society Annual Report, 1980, Kensington and Chelsea Local Studies Collection, 050CHEL, p. 10.

7   Peter York, 'Culture as Commodity: Star Wars, Punk and Pageant', in *Design after Modernism*, ed. John Thackera (London, 1987), p. 161.

8   Peter Saville, 'Post-Los Angeles Postmodern', *Eye* (Summer 1995), online resource.

9   Dylan Jones, 'People are Seduced by Fabric: Interview with Scott Crolla', *i-D Magazine*, 22 (February 1985).

10   Colin McDowell, *Man of Fashion: Peacock Males and Perfect Gentlemen* (London, 1997), p. 201.

CHAPTER EIGHT

1.   Stephen Willats, *Between Buildings and People* (London, 1996), p. 77.

2   T. S. Eliot, *The Waste Land and Other Poems* (London, 1972), p. 23.

3   Emma Dexter, 'Picturing the City', in *Century City* (London, 2000), p. 75.

4   Sarah Kent, *Shark Infested Waters* (London, 1994), p. 39.

5   Caroline Evans, *Fashion at the Edge* (London, 2003), p. 11.

6   In *The City Cultures Reader*, ed. M. Miles, T. Hall and I. Borden (London, 2000), p. 140.

7   Val Williams, *Hannah Starkey*, exh. cat., Dublin (2000).

Agar, Eileen, with Andrew Lambirth, *A Look at My Life* (London, 1988)
—, manuscript for autobiography, 2 January 1985, Tate Archive 911.38
Altick, Richard D., *The Shows of London* (Cambridge, MA, 1978)
Arnold, Rebecca, *Fashion, Desire and Anxiety: Image and Morality in the 21st Century* (London, 2001)
Bailey, Peter, 'Parasexuality and Glamour: The Victorian Barmaid as Cultural Prototype', *Gender and History*, II/2 (Summer 1990), pp. 148–54
Banting, John, *A Blue Book of Conversation* (London, 1946)
Beaton, Cecil, *The Glass of Fashion* (London, 1954)
—, sketchbooks, Archive of Art and Design, London
Beckson, Karl, *London in the 1890s: A Cultural History* (New York and London, 1992)
Berger, John, *About Looking* (London, 1980)
Berman, Marshall, *All That Is Solid Melts into Air: The Experience of Modernity* (London, 1983)
Blazwick, Iwona, ed., *An Endless Passion, An Endless Banquet: A Situationist Scrapbook* (London, 1989)
Blum, Dilys E., *Shocking! The Art and Fashion of Elsa Schiaparelli*, exh. cat., Philadelphia Museum of Art (New Haven and London, 2004)
Blunt, Reginald, *The Wonderful Village: A Further Record of Some Famous Folk and Places by Chelsea Reach* (London, 1918)
Booker, Christopher, *The Neophiliacs* (London, 1969)
Bracewell, Michael, *The Nineties: When Surface Was Depth* (London, 2002)
Breward, Christopher, *The Hidden Consumer: Masculinities, Fashion and City Life, 1860–1914* (Manchester, 1999)
Brilliant!: New Art From London, exh. cat., Walker Arts Centre, Contemporary Arts Museum (Houston, TX, 1996)
Bromberg, Craig, *The Wicked Ways of Malcolm McLaren* (London, 1991)
Buck, Louisa, *The Surrealist Spirit in Britain* (London, 1988)
Buck-Morss, Susan, *The Dialectics of Seeing: Walter Benjamin and the Arcades Project* (Cambridge, MA, 1989)
Burchett, George, *Memoirs of a Tattooist* (London, 1958)
Burkitt, Ian, *Bodies of Thought: Embodiment, Identity and Modernity* (London, 1999)
Burnard, Joyce, *Chintz and Cotton* (Kenthurst, NSW, 1984)
Celant, Germano, 'The Transparency of Architecture', in *Langlands & Bell*, exh. cat., Serpentine Gallery (London, 1996)
Chambers, Iain, 'Maps for the Metropolis: A Portable Guide to the Present', *Cultural Studies*, I/1 (January 1987)
—, *Popular Culture: The Metropolitan Experience* (London, 1986)

—, 'Narratives of Nationalism: Being "British"', in *Space and Place: Theories of Identity and Location*, ed. Erica Carter, James Donald and Judith Squires (London, 1993)

Chenoune, Farid, *A History of Men's Fashion* (Paris, 1993)

Chodzko, Adam, *Adam Chodzko* (London, 1999)

Cohn, Nik, *Today There Are No Gentlemen: The Changes in Englishmen's Clothes since the War* (London, 1971)

Coley, Frederick C., *The Turkish Bath: Its History and Its Uses* (London, 1887)

Cooper, Jeremy, *No Fun Without U: The Art of Factual Nonsense* (London, 2000)

Core, Philip, *Camp: The Lie That Tells the Truth* (London, 1984)

Cork, Richard, *Vorticism and Abstract Art in the Age of the Machine*, exh. cat., Hayward Gallery (London, 1974)

Dakers, Caroline, *The Holland Park Circle: Artists and Victorian Society* (New Haven and London, 1999)

Deakin, John, *London Today* (London, 1949)

Debord, Guy, *The Society of the Spectacle* (New York, 1994)

De Certeau, Michel, *The Practice of Everyday Life* (Berkeley, CA, 1984)

De la Haye, Amy, *The Cutting Edge: 50 Years of British Fashion, 1947–1997*, exh. cat., Victoria and Albert Museum (London, 1997)

Dexter, Emma, ed., *Century City*, exh. cat., Tate Modern (London, 2000)

The Citibank Private Bank Photography Prize 2001: In Association with the Photographer's Gallery, exh. cat., The Photographer's Gallery (London, 2001)

Dixon Hunt, John, *The Pre-Raphaelite Imagination, 1848–1900* (London, 1968)

Donald, James, *Imagining the Modern City* (London, 1999)

Doy, Gen, *Drapery: Classicism and Barbarism in Visual Culture* (London, 2002)

Duff Gordon, Lady, *Discretions and Indiscretions* (New York, 1932)

Dunn, Henry T., *Recollections of D. G. Rossetti and his Circle* (London, 1904)

Eliot, T. S., *The Wasteland* (1922), in *Selected Poems* (London, 1954)

Etherington-Smith, Meredith, and Jeremy Pilcher, *The 'It' Girls: Lucy, Lady Duff Gordon, the Couturière 'Lucile' and Elinor Glyn* (London, 1986)

Evans, Caroline, 'The Enchanted Spectacle', in *Fashion Theory*, v/3 (August 2001), pp. 271–310

—, *Fashion at the Edge: Spectacle, Modernity and Deathliness* (New Haven and London, 2003)

—, and Minna Thornton, *Women and Fashion: A New Look* (London, 1989)

Farson, Daniel *The Gilded Gutter Life of Francis Bacon* (London, 1993)

Fer, Briony, 'The Hat, the Hoax, the Body', in *The Body Imaged: The Human Form and Visual Culture since the Renaissance*, ed. Kathleen Adler and Marcia Pointon (Cambridge, 1993), pp. 161–74

Fletcher, Donald, *Tattooing among Civilized People: Read Before the Anthropological Society of Washington* (19 December 1882)

Gertner Zatlin, Linda, *Beardsley, Japonisme and the Perversion of the Victorian Ideal* (Cambridge, 1997)

Glyn, Anthony, *Elinor Glyn: A Biography* (London, 1955)

Goddard, Donald, *Blimey! Another Book about London* (London, 1974)

Gordon, Jan, and Cora Gordon, *The London Roundabout* (Bombay and Sydney, 1933)

Gray, Christopher, *Leaving the 20th Century: The Incomplete work of the Situationist International* (London, 1998)

Green, Jonathan, *All Dressed Up: The Sixties and the Counterculture* (London, 1999)

Greenhalgh, Paul, *Ephemeral Vistas* (Manchester, 1988)

Grimes, Teresa, Judith Collins and Oriana Baddeley, *Five Women Painters* (Oxford, 1984)

Hannah Starkey, exh. cat., Museum of Modern Art (Dublin, 2000)

Harris, Wendell V., 'An Anatomy of Aestheticism', in *Victorian Literature and Society: Essays Presented to Richard D. Altick*, ed. James R. Kincaid and Albert J. Kuhn (Columbus, OH, 1984)

Haughton, Edward, *The Uses and Abuses of the Turkish Bath* (London, 1861)

Hebdige, Dick, *Subculture: The Meaning of Style* (London, 1988)

Hibbert, H., *Fifty Years of a Londoner's Life* (London, 1916)

Hill, Paul, and Thomas Cooper, *Dialogue with Photography* (Manchester, 1992)

Huysmans, J. K., *Against Nature* (Oxford, 1998)

International Surrealist Bulletin, 4 (June 1936)

Jackson, Stanley, *Indiscreet Guide to Soho* (London, 1946)

Jameson, Frederick, 'Cognitive Mapping', in *The Jameson Reader*, ed. Michael Hardt and Kathi Weeks (Oxford, 2000), pp. 277–87

—, 'Postmodernism; or, The Logic of Late Capitalism', in *The Jameson Reader* ed. Michael Hardt and Kathi Weeks (Oxford, 2000), pp. 188–232

Kaplan, Joel H., and Sheila Stowell, *Theatre and Fashion: Oscar Wilde to the Suffragettes* (London, 1994)

Kennett, Frances, *The Collector's Book of Twentieth-Century Fashion* (London, 1983)

Kent, Sarah, *Shark Infested Waters* (London, 1994)

Kracauer, Siegfried, 'The Hotel Lobby', in his *Mass Ornament: Weimar Essays* (London, 1995)

Krauss, Rosalind, *The Originality of the Avant-Garde and Other Modernist Myths* (Cambridge, MA, 1985)

Lefevbre, Henri, *The Critique of Everyday Life: Volume 1* (London and New York, 1991)

—, 'Plan of the Present Work', from 'The Production of Space' (1991), in *The City Cultures Reader*, ed. Malcolm Miles, Tim Hall and Iain Borden (London, 2004), pp. 260–65

Lehmann, Ulrich, *Tigersprung: Fashion in Modernity* (London, 2000)

Lesser, Wendy, *His Other Half: Man Looking at Women Through Art* (Cambridge, MA, 1991)

Light Box, exh. cat., The Architectural Association (London, 1985)

Lipovetsky, Gilles, *The Empire of Fashion: Dressing Modern Democracy* (Princeton, NJ, 1994)

Lombroso, Cesar, *The Criminal Man in Relation to Anthropology, Jurisprudence and Prison Discipline* (1878)

Loos, Adolf, 'Ornament and Crime', in *Ornament and Crime: Selected Essays* (Riverside, CA, 1998)

Maclaren Ross, Julian, *Memoirs of the Forties* (London, 1965)

Marcus, Greil, *Lipstick Traces* (London, 1989)

Martin, Richard, *Fashion and Surrealism* (London, 1988)

Mellor, David, ed., *Beaton*, exh. cat., Barbican Art Gallery (London, 1986)

Melly, George, *Revolt into Style: The Pop Arts in Britain* (Harmondsworth, 1972)

Mifflin, Margot, *Bodies of Subversion: A Secret History of Women and Tattoo* (New York, 1997)

Mort, Frank, *Cultures of Consumption: Masculinities and Social Space in Late Twentieth Century Britain* (London, 1996)

Murray, Jacqueline, ed., *Mappa Mundi: Mapping Culture/Mapping the World* (Windsor, ONT, 2001)

Nead, Lynda, *Victorian Babylon: People, Streets and Images in 19th Century London* (New Haven and London, 2000)

Nehring, Neil, *Flowers in the Dustbin* (Ann Arbor, MI, 1993)

Nord, Deborah Epstein, 'The Social Explorer as Anthropologist', in *Visions of the Modern City*, ed. William Sharpe and Leonard Wallock (London, 1987), pp. 122–34

Peiss, Kathy, 'Making Up, Making Over: Cosmetics, Consumer Culture and Women's Identities', in *The Sex of Things: Gender and Consumption in Historical Perspective*, ed. Victoria de Grazia and Ellen Furlough (Berkeley, CA, 1996), pp. 311–66

Penrose, Roland, *Eileen Agar: A Decade of Discoveries*, exh. cat., New Art Centre (London, 1976)

—, photographs of Surrealist albums, Conway Library, Courtauld Institute of Art, 1848A

Peppiatt, Michael, *Francis Bacon: Anatomy of an Enigma* (Boulder, CO, 1998)

Pile, Steve, *The Body and the City: Psychoanalysis, Space and Subjectivity* (London, 1995)

—, and Nigel Thrift, eds, *Mapping the Subject: Geographies of Cultural*

Transformation (London, 1995)

Polan, Brenda, *The Fashion Year* (London, 1983)

Purdy, D. W., *Tattooing: How to Tattoo, What To Use and How To Use Them* (London, 1896)

Quant, Mary, *Quant by Quant* (London, 1966)

Raban, Jonathan, *Soft City* (London, 1974)

Rappaport, Erika Diane, *Shopping for Pleasure: Women in the Making of London's West End* (Princeton, NJ, 2000)

Read, Herbert, *Eileen Agar: Retrospective Exhibition of Paintings and Collages, 1930–64*, exh. cat., Brook Street Gallery (London, 1964)

Reid, Jamie, *Up They Rise: The Incomplete Works of Jamie Reid* (London, 1987)

Remy, Michael, *Surrealism in Britain* (Aldershot, 1999)

Rendell, Jane, 'Displaying Sexuality: Gendered Identities and the Early Nineteenth Century', in *Images of the Street: Planning, Identity and Control In Public Space*, ed. Nicholas R. Fyfe (London, 1998), pp. 75–91

Richardson, Nigel, *Dog Days in Soho: One Man's Adventures in 1950s Bohemia* (London, 2000)

Rita [pseudonym], *The Mystery of a Turkish Bath* (London, 1888)

Roberts, James, 'Never Had it So Good', in *General Release*, exh. cat., 46th Venice Biennale (1995)

Samuel, Raphael, *Theatres of Memory* (London, 1994)

Saville, Peter, interviewed by Rick Poyner, *Eye* (Summer 1995)

Schiaparelli, Elsa, *Shocking Life* (London, 1954)

Schivelbusch, Wolfgang, *Disenchanted Night: The Industrialization of Light in the Nineteenth Century* (Berg, 1988)

Schwartz, Frederick, 'Commodity Signs: Peter Behrens, the AEG and the Trademark', *Journal of Design History*, IX/3 (1996)

Simmel, Georg, *On Individuality and Social Forms*, ed. Donald N. Levine (Chicago, 1973)

Simpson, Ann, David Gascoyne and Andrew Lambirth, *Eileen Agar, 1899–1991*, exh. cat., Scottish National Gallery of Modern Art (Edinburgh, 1991)

Sims, George K., ed., *Living London*, vol. II, pt 2 (London, 1903)

Solomon-Godeau, Abigail, 'The Other Side of Venus', in *The Sex of Things: Gender and Consumption in Historical Perspective*, ed. Victoria de Grazia and Ellen Furlough (Berkeley, CA, 1996), pp. 113–50

Surrealism: Desire Unbound, exh. cat., Tate Modern (London, 2001)

Surrealist Objects and Poems, exh. cat., London Gallery (London, 1937)

Sylvester, David, *Interviews with Francis Bacon* (London, 1987)

Trollope, Anthony, 'The Turkish Bath', in *Novels and Stories* (London, 1946)

Tzara, Tristan, 'Of a Certain Automatism of Taste', *Le Minotaure*, III (1933)

Urquhart, David, *The Pillars of Hercules; or, A Narrative of Travels in Spain and Morocco in 1848* (London, 1850)

Van Alphen, Ernst, *Francis Bacon and the Loss of Self* (London, 1992)

Vaughan, Keith, *Keith Vaughan Diaries: Journals, 1939–1977* (London, 1989)

Vermorel, Fred, *Fashion and Perversity: A Life of Vivienne Westwood and the Sixties Laid Bare* (London, 1997)

—, and Judy Vermorel, *The Sex Pistol: The Inside Story* (London, 1987)

Walker, John A., *Cross Currents: Art into Pop, Pop into Art* (London, 1987)

Watanabe, Toshio, 'High Victorian Japonisme', *Swiss Asian Studies: Research Studies*, vol. x (Bern, 1991)

Weightman, Gavin, *Bright Light, Big City: London Entertained, 1830–1950* (London, 1992)

Westwood, Sallie, and John Williams, eds, *Imagining Cities: Scripts, Signs, Memory* (London, 1997)

Wiener, Martin J., *English Culture and the Decline of the Industrial Spirit, 1850–1980* (London, 1982)

Willats, Stephen, *City of Concrete*, exh. cat., Ikon Gallery (Birmingham, 1986)

—, *Between Buildings and People* (London, 1996)

Williams, Rosalind, *Dream Worlds: Mass Consumption in Late 19th Century France* (Berkeley, CA, 1982)

Wilson, Elizabeth, *The Sphinx in the City: Urban Life, the Control of Disorder and Women* (London, 1991)

Winner, Gerd, *Kelpra Studio*, exh. cat., Drumcroon Arts Centre (Wigan, 1981)

Wishart, Michael, *High Diver* (London, 1977)

Woolf, Virginia, *The London Scene: Five Essays by Virginia Woolf* (London, 1975)

York, Peter, *The Eighties* (London, 1993)

—, 'Culture as Commodity: Style Wars, Punk and Pageant', in *Design after Modernism*, ed. John Thackeray (London, 1987), pp. 160–68

I would like to give special thanks to Caroline Evans for first suggesting I contact Reaktion about the possibility of publishing a book, for reading and responding to the manuscript so willingly and wisely, and for facilitating funding from the Arts & Humanities Research Council through the research project *Fashion and Modernity*. This included access to a picture researcher, so I would also like to thank Marketa Uhlirova for tirelessly sourcing illustrations and negotiating reproduction fees. I must also credit Catharina Holmberg for her translation of a Tristan Tzara article.

I am also grateful to colleagues at London College of Fashion and Central Saint Martins, notably Sonia Ashmore, Christopher Breward, Adam Briggs, Judith Clark, Jo Entwistle, Shelley Fox, Pamela Church Gibson, Kitty Hauser, Amy de la Haye, Rob Lutton, Helen Thomas, Elizabeth Wilson and Val Williams. Last but not least, I would like to thank Patrick Haragdon.

PHOTO ACKNOWLEDGEMENTS

The author and publishers wish to express their thanks to the following sources of illustrative material and/or permission to reproduce it.

Photo author: p. 107; photos British Film Institute: pp. 9, 10; photos the British Library, Colindale: pp. 31, 33; Cecil Beaton/Vogue Conde Nast Publications Inc.: p. 82; photo courtesy John Culme, Footlight Notes Collection: p. 69; photos John Deakin/Vogue © The Conde Nast Publications Ltd.: pp. 103, 115, 122; Fox Photos/Getty Images: p. 164 (top); photo Fergus Greer: p. 16; photos Guildhall Library, Corporation of London: pp. 28, 29; photo courtesy of The Hollywood Renegades Archive [www.cobbles.com]: p. 63; Collection of Huddersfield Art Gallery (presented by the Contemporary Art Society to Batley Art Gallery, 1952), photo Huddersfield Art Gallery: p. 109; photos courtesy of the artist (Hannah Starkey), courtesy Maureen Paley/Interim Art (London): pp. 218, 221; photo James Jackson/© Getty Images/Hulton Archive: p. 112; photo courtesy of the Jersey Heritage Trust, St Helier, Jersey (© Jersey Heritage Trust): p. 15; photo Kensington & Chelsea Archives: p. 164 (foot); courtesy Lisson Gallery, London: pp. 201, 207; reproduced by permission of the London Metropolitan Archives (published by the GLC, Crown Copyright reserved): p. 176; photos © Niall McIrnerney: pp. 11, 17, 158, 168, 170, 180, 181, 182, 191; © Man Ray Trust/ADAGP, Paris and DACS, London 2004: p. 83; Manchester City Art Galleries: p. 172; photo Donald Milne: p. 209; Motif Editions, London: p. 165; Museum of Costume, Bath: p. 20; Museum of London (photo Museum of London): p. 58; photo © Tim Noble and Sue Webster, courtesy Modern Art, London: p. 215; Oxford Illustrators: p. 154; Pale Green Press: p. 198; Austin Reed Group plc.: p. 136; photo © RMN/R.G. Ojeda: p. 43 (Musée Gustave Moreau, Paris); from Tom Salter, Carnaby Street (London, 1970), p. 126; Salvador Dalí/Vogue © Condé Nast Publications, Inc.: p. 91 (top); Salvador Dalí Museum, St Petersburg, Florida (photo Salvador Dalí Museum): p. 91 (foot); courtesy Sanderson: p. 184; photo courtesy of the Sho Gallery: p. 167; courtesy of Sotheby's: p. 88; photos Terrence Spencer/© Time LifePictures/Getty Images: pp. 149, 150; Tate Britain, London: p. 42 (photo © Tate, London 2004); photos courtesy of the Tate Archive: pp. 73, 77, 80, 93, 96, 110 (© holder c/o Marlborough Fine Art), 117 (Isabel Rawsthorne Archive, © Nicholas Warwick), 121 (Isabel Rawsthorne Archive); photo courtesy of the Tattoo Archive, Berkeley, CA: p. 47; courtesy of the Tattoo Club of Great Britain, Oxford: pp. 48, 49; courtesy Juergen Teller: p. 210; photo © The Trustees of the Edward James Foundation: p. 94; photo Marketa Uhlirova (courtesy of Marco Pirroni): p. 160; Victoria & Albert Museum, London (photos V&A Images/Victoria & Albert Museum): pp. 66, 97; photos V&A Images/Victoria & Albert Museum: 129 (photo Colin Davey for Camera Press), 130, 131, 138, 139–140 (Archive of Art & Design, John Stephen Archive), 143 (photo Hamish Campbell for Scotsman Publications), 151, 153 (photo Colin Davey for Camera Press); photos Westminster City Archives: pp. 36, 50, 51; photos Westminster City Archives/GOAD: p. 26 (GOAD sheet 208), 72 (GOAD sheet 216), 100 (Sheet FIP IX.226); photo Richard White: p. 187; courtesy of the artist (Gary Hume) & Jay Jopling/White Cube (London), photos © the artist: pp. 206, 214.